A COMEDY & A TRAGEDY

Ballantine Books New York

A COMEDY & A TRAGEDY

A Memoir of Learning How to Read and Write

Travis Hugh Culley

Published in the United States by Ballantine Books,
an imprint of Random House, a division of
Penguin Random House LLC, New York.

BALLANTINE and the HOUSE colophon are registered
trademarks of Penguin Random House LLC.

Special thanks to New World School of the Arts, the School
of the Art Institute of Chicago, Ox-Bow, the Wings Foundation,
and the SNAP Network. Extended appreciation to John A. Ware,
Mary Jane Jacob, Kelly Bristol-Bell, Richard P. Janaro,
Megan Hickling, Sylvan Seidenman, Shirley Meyers,
Debbie Holle, Emily Svaedra, and Mary Wolf.

LIBRARY OF CONGRESS CATALOGING-IN-PUBLICATION DATA
Culley, Travis Hugh.
A comedy & a tragedy: a memoir of learning how to read and write /
Travis Hugh Culley.
pages cm
ISBN 978-0-345-50616-0
eBook ISBN 978-0-8041-7755-9
1. Culley, Travis Hugh—Childhood and youth. 2. Reading, Psychology of.
3. Writing—Psychological aspects. 4. Literacy—Psychological aspects.
5. Problem youth—United States—Biography. I. Title.
II. Title: A comedy and a tragedy.
BF456.R2C85 2015
818'.603—dc23 2015000866
[B]

Printed in the United States of America on acid-free paper

randomhousebooks.com

2 4 6 8 9 7 5 3 1

FIRST EDITION

Book design by Mary A. Wirth
Frontispiece photograph and journal illustration
courtesy of the author

For Aneta Szklanko

We cannot teach children the danger of lying to men
Without feeling, as men,
The greater danger of lying to children.

—JEAN-JACQUES ROUSSEAU

CONTENTS

PREFACE

Dear Aneta,

On September 21, 2005, I was a graduate student at the School of the Art Institute of Chicago on assignment in Finland to write about an arts festival that takes place there every year. On my way home, before flying out of Helsinki, I stepped into an English-language bookstore near the center of town. It is here we met.

Two tiny rooms were connected by one small set of stairs. Worn volumes with colorful spines lined the walls and shelves and were, in places, stacked to the ceiling. I was reading the introduction of an out-of-print anthology of papers on the sociology of art that I'd found at the bottom of the reference section. You were scanning mass-market paperbacks in the yellow discount bin. A delicate-looking man sat near the front and gave change as customers made their selections and left. Unavoidably, I came up beside you. There was no cause for alarm. It seemed you were expecting me.

Being polite, I thumbed through a weathered copy of *The*

Fall by Albert Camus. I saw your fingers tapping the edge of the bin like a family of little dancers.

"Have you seen Jane?" you asked, with a faintly English accent.

"Jane Austen? Jane Jacobs? Jane Smiley?"

"I've been looking for an English edition of *Pride and Prejudice* for years."

You weren't English, and you were dark for a Finn. "I haven't seen her," I said. "But then I haven't checked the fiction shelf."

"Have you read *Pride*?" you asked.

"I know of her books, of course. I haven't read them."

"You haven't?"

"I'm sure they're wonderful." I smiled. "But I don't have time to read just for the pleasure of it."

"Don't you enjoy reading?"

"Yes, I do. But *pleasure* is not my first motivation," I said with a laugh, trying to clarify.

"Why do you read?"

"Ideas, I guess. Ideas do play some part in my interest in reading." I worried that I was sounding pretentious. "I think I am responsible to the ideas I find in books. That's why I read them." Then I said something about the similarity between literature and philosophy.

"You mean like Hermes and Aphrodite?"

"Like Mercury. Ideas are not things, right? Not in themselves. But they seem so solid sometimes, so absolutely sound, so like real things. It is the same with a work of fiction."

"It can be revealing?"

"Reading will unveil illusions. And yet still, there is always some work that goes into making sure that what you read—*however it seems to you*—is in fact what the author meant to write. Maybe I never learned to enjoy the process the way others have. I love books. I study books. But I read them because I have to, not because I expect them to be *pleasant*."

"You have to learn?"

"I guess I'm a slow learner."

You looked up. I didn't seem like a slow learner.

"It's true. For most of my time in school, I didn't read or write at all. In middle school I was called a problem because I never followed directions. By high school I was against any and all rules whatsoever."

"You were illiterate?"

"Until about seventeen."

"What happened?"

I flipped through Stephen King's *Insomnia* and then set it back into the space it occupied. I wasn't sure what to say because we had only met, and people come with so many different prejudices about literacy. I said, "It may be hard to imagine, but it is fairly normal in my country for students to graduate high school without the ability to read or write."

"Were you dyslexic?"

"I am, somewhat, but it's not severe. It doesn't keep me from reading. My challenges were social, environmental, and emotional. I grew up in inner-city schools in South Florida. Both of my parents were educated, with master's degrees. I should have had every chance and all of the potential to read like other kids, but—" I took a breath. "There was no support. Parents got in the way. Teachers got in the way. By the fourth grade, I couldn't trust anyone. *Why would I want to learn what they had to teach me?* I refused. I thought, if I agreed to their terms, I'd only agree to being lied to."

You cracked a smile.

"As a kid, I thought I only had to speak my mind and would never really have to write anything down. If I didn't need to write anything down, why bother reading? Anyway, the world doesn't attend so carefully to the names of things, even now. We don't call things by what they are. This can be confusing. Ultimately, it was in art school that I discovered the meaning of and purpose in literacy. I learned I needed to write and I needed to read in order to understand my own situation. Once I'd figured this out, I became a writer. Nothing could stop me."

"Were you an artist?"

"I was in the theater. In fact, plays were an important introduction to reading for me. Surrounded by actors, each with the play in hand, I could call for help on words I did not know or could not pronounce. The others would let me fumble through a scene with them until I figured it out. Reading in collaboration this way, in a group, I developed the ability to read different kinds of parts and experiment with more sophisticated plays. When I began reading books, I found it helpful to imagine the narration coming from someone onstage."

"That's creative."

"I came to literacy late, and it was the theater that brought me. Oh yes." I'd forgotten. "I began a journal." I reached into my bag for money. I paid for *The Fall,* and the essays on the sociology of art. Before leaving, we exchanged names. You told me you were not Finnish but Polish, here on a student visa. You were studying English philology at seminary. I took interest. I had never talked with a philologist about literature. I welcomed the conversation as we took a walk in the street outside.

First, you asked what novelists I enjoyed. I named a few writers: Dostoyevsky, Primo Levi, Borges, and Melville. "I sometimes lack patience with novels," I had to admit. "The moment a writer seems distracted, I become distracted. If I find something else more interesting, I can be fickle. I might put one book down and start another, but then *I'm working.*"

"What do you enjoy reading?"

"I like reading about the real and imagined world. I love all sorts of essayists, poets, playwrights, thinkers, regardless of their origins or their belief systems. I have a special appreciation for literary criticism, books about writing. I have a soft spot for phenomenology."

"*Ideas*?" you asked cautiously. "And what are *ideas* good for?"

It seemed that you were serious, so I attempted some reply. "Ideas help me to reflect and to sort out chaos. A good idea can help organize all the information that is available at one time. Ideas give me a way of understanding something that, up front, may not make perfect sense, or may be too complex to see from a single point of view." I thought I had said something profound here, but then you asked another question:

"How do you *become* literate?"

I saw you speak, but I had lost the ability to understand what you were saying. I rocked back and forth in my shoes, unsure of how to explain. I stammered, foolishly: "I've written one book and a couple of articles. I have a pile of journals, a handful of plays."

You asked the question again: "How do you *become* literate?" I think you expected me to have an answer; I expected you to have one. We talked for a long time. We enjoyed a beautiful day together, but we couldn't seem to reach an agreement.

In the time that has passed since that day, I have been collecting a more complete reply to your question. My story will describe what I could not explain adequately that day: how I learned to read, and how I came to be a writer after the prolonged illiteracy of my childhood.

A COMEDY & A TRAGEDY

CHAPTER ONE

Birdbrain

I looked out the window of my dad's brown van, watching trees pass by. My mom and brother, Joe, were strapped in behind their seat belts, waving goodbye to the mountains in the rearview mirror. It was the spring of 1980, and we were driving from Denver, Colorado, to Miami, Florida. A truck filled with furniture and clothes drove east a few hours ahead of us.

Feeling the van rock side to side, I caught myself staring at miles of wheat and corn, barbed-wire fences, and occasional bales of hay. Looking ahead, smelling the pine and horses, feeling the wind carry, I felt that my life was changing. Houses peered out at us and vanished. Once fascinated,

I had to wonder where they went. Whole towns disappeared, never to be seen again. One moment I saw cabbages, radio towers, farms, and then empty stretches of road.

Weeks before, Joe and I had been taken out of school to prepare for our move back east. Joe was in the third grade. I was in the first. Before our move I asked him, thinking he knew better, how things would be different in Florida. He looked around at the schoolyard where we stood:

"Everything will be different."

We moved into a neighborhood house with an acre yard that sat back from the shoulder of a busy two-lane street in North Miami. The house was spacious and open. The walls were paneled with stained wood. The hall creaked and moaned. There was a porch at the front of the house and an enclosed swimming pool in the back. The screens whistled differently in the warm wind. The windows were glass venetian-style shutters, thin plates that we opened and closed with little metal dials. Each window was covered by an awning, and so the house was always dark within, even when we had every light on. Dad thought we had no room to complain. With a pool and a backyard like ours, he was sure Joe and I had everything we should need.

Dad warned us that we would soon be going to a bigger school, and that we'd need to prepare ourselves. First of all, Miami was nothing like the suburbs of Denver. Here, we'd be taking classes with people from all over the world. We'd have to learn to talk with different kinds of people, and even deal with the sense of being a minority in some of our classrooms, although this, he suggested, wasn't really true and would in time wear off. Passing tests and turning in assignments should be easy. The problem would be the jealousy of other boys, he said. At school, kids would envy us because we were luckier than they. He had this phrase: *most likely to succeed*.

Here began two very different journeys in education. My brother would become an honors student, earning high marks and graduating easily. I would be called a discipline problem. My path would be beset with many obstacles, and I would remain illiterate until high school.

♦ ♦ ♦

When our mother brought us in to register for classes, it was March, only nine weeks from the end of the school year. She parked the Pinto on the street and led us into Biscayne Gardens Elementary through a side door. Together, we found ourselves in a desolate hall that seemed to have no end and, for the moment, only one boy standing halfway down the expanse of classrooms, facing the wall. Mom walked up to the boy and asked him where the principal's office was. The boy spun but did not answer. Instead, he held his breath, blowing his cheeks out like a blowfish, and pointed farther up the hall.

"Why are you holding your breath?" I asked him. He was my age.

"I'm in trouble," he said, inflating.

"What for?"

"Talking in class," he peeped, his shoulders high.

I looked to my mom: *You can't talk in these classrooms?* But then he laughed and I laughed and we were friends. This was Bruce Melvin Woolever, Jr. As luck would have it, I would be placed in his first-grade class. He and I would follow each other, hopscotch, through the next ten years, depending on each other at some of the hardest turns.

Bruce and I were nothing alike. He came from a busy home with three younger sisters. His father was Italian, his mother Guatemalan. He was *mixed,* he said, in quotes. At home they spoke Spanish and English interchangeably, and were probably more literate in each language than I was in my own. Bruce didn't feel superior about this. The world was big enough for all kinds of people. His perspective was admirable. He said that everyone had something to laugh about. Even those people who don't want to laugh at all or find any joke funny ever—even *they* have something to laugh about. He laughed himself silly saying this.

Unlike me, Bruce had little shame getting attention. Unlike my brother, he was gentle and motivated by sympathy. Bruce was never hurtful. He did not see stereotypes or respond to clichés. To him, things were funny in themselves. I could give some turn to a phrase and he would take it straight: "My brother is going to *get it* someday, I swear."

"Get it? Get what? Oh! I get it—I got it!" Then he'd fake like I'd hit him and stagger back. He always cheered me up. Over lunch, he'd try to trade food. Once, he stuck a finger in my cornbread and asked if I wanted to eat it.

"That's gross!"

"Aren't you *touchy*?" He chortled, his mouth full of my cornbread.

I let it go. I needed Bruce's friendship more than he needed mine. I was the younger brother of Joe Culley, a bully, twice my size, who had taken up the art of condescension. Compared to Bruce's, my brother's sense of humor consisted only of potshots and double crossings, inspired by *Spy vs Spy*. Joe defended himself. He wasn't being cruel; he was only exhibiting his knack for competition. Joe loved competition because it established unarguable authority—but then there he was, my older brother, parading his authority through the house. Joe brought home perfect report cards, 4.0 averages. He gloated about being superior to me in every aspect, even over the two inches he maintained above me as Mom marked our heights up on the pantry door. There it was: *Black spy—wins again!*

Joe was also the senior book lover in the family. I think that by nine he'd read more books than both of our parents combined. He wasn't dumb, but *mean*. He enjoyed mysteries, fantasies, especially the sci-fi and horror genres. As a boy, he'd read the Hardy Boys and Agatha Christie. Now he was reading Stephen King and Ian Fleming. It seemed he didn't read these books for any virtuous reason, but only to deepen his twisted mind—to see what he could get away with. He wanted facts, science, information he could use or take advantage of. I didn't want to be anything like him. I think it bruised his ego.

At home, Joe let it be known that I was the gullible one, the *dummy*. He called me know-nothing, nitwit, dork. He called me Birdbrain so often that I eventually flew into a fit, and the name stuck. Joe earned his nickname when he pinned me to the ground in the backyard and sat on my head like King Kong. He was trying to impress a friend from the football league who was standing right there, speechless. Mom and Dad couldn't hear me calling for help. I started yelling,

"You're a butt! Nothing but a fat butt!" Afterward, every time he called me one name I called him the other.

"Birdbrain."

"Yes, *Butt*?"

"Don't call me that!"

To me, it didn't matter that he could read books. In my mind, he was just getting fat behind those stubby, gray paperbacks. I mean, books were for lazy people, *obviously,* and people who didn't have better things to do. I wanted to *do* things. I loved sports, and action movies. I was not afraid of danger. I had messy hair that formed little wings over my ears, and a dusting of freckles on my cheeks. I was the kid who would always take a dare.

Joe said he liked this about me. In some way, he liked that about the authors he read. They were fearless, they *did* things. Still, I could not get past the idea of having someone else's words stuck in my head where I couldn't reach them, or change them, or determine what other words they might lead to. He said that was the dumbest thing he'd ever heard.

Once, Joe dared me to read. He brought me to the horror novels on his bookshelf. I grabbed one and flipped the pages. I grabbed another. "What's the difference? They're all the same. Every page is just like every other!"

We separated in disagreement.

On my own, when I tried to read, I found myself instantly exhausted, easily distracted, and constantly unsure of what I was supposed to be doing. Each word looked like a broken collection of figures that had once been orderly and carefully arranged—like coats that had once been hung up in a closet. When I looked down, the coats were in disarray. All of the letters had fallen out of the words and into a heap at the bottom of the page. Words were only a way of seeing the alphabet in ruins. How could I fit my whole life, beginning, middle, and end, through such a misshapen form as this?

If I opened a book, I didn't see sentences, only parts of phrases, and assorted sounds; ropes, balls, trees. But with every word and line jammed up beside every other, who knew how this noise was all supposed to sound? When I read a name, even in one line of a story, I lost track of what they were doing in the next line—or on the next page. I followed clues in just about every direction but then found myself deafened, and staring. Reading didn't get me anywhere, and it did not fulfill my need for stories.

The idea that reading opened the mind seemed totally backward to me; the opposite was more likely. Written words seemed to have the effect of framing the mind, narrowing options. They were only one step away from mind control—as I saw it—or brainwashing. Words were limits, boundaries. How could they lead to *everything*?

In Mrs. Wyndham's class I kept my concerns to myself. I feared speaking up because I thought I might crack and then try to say whatever there was room to say. Why are there only so many letters in the alphabet, not fewer? Not more? Why do some words have only one letter? What is the real story of the alphabet? Why does *f* follow *e,* and *n* follow *m,* and *u* lead to *w,* as it clearly does? I thought, *I can't speak up about this. I'd only be told to stand outside and face the wall.*

The next year, Bruce and I would no longer share the same classroom. Mrs. Pickard, my new teacher, found me to be a joyful and optimistic boy. In January, on the Stanford

Achievement Tests for grade schools, I received above-average scores: 66 percent in listening, 94 percent in math computation. I was below average, earning only 48 percent, in reading comprehension. There was still every hope of my being able to learn how to read.

CHAPTER TWO

Why Feathers Give Me Headaches

Teachers say that literacy starts in the family. If that's true, then I came from two families. There was the family that thought itself highly educated, fully functional, and yet this was the same family that thought it wasn't up to them to teach me how to read. Unlike other children, I have no memory of my father or mother reading books. I don't recall being read stories. I don't have favorite characters or myths that I identified with at an early age. Seldom did anyone write to me, or expect to receive my thoughts in writing. It didn't bother anyone that I couldn't read.

There was, in our family, some importance given to documents. To my parents, written words were considered weightier than mere spoken expressions. Writing was reserved for serious business like school assignments, legal judgments, tickets, a license to practice, a schedule of classes. Promises, degrees, laws, these required keeping track of. Stories were hardly necessary. They were more like distractions from the events we screened on television.

Where it came to literacy itself, there was really no illiterate option. This is why, early on, I was not called by that name either. Mom believed there was always a name for a thing—you only had to know where to look. In her mind, the world had already been figured out and that's why we had books. She didn't expect me to take an interest in reading them. I was too easily distracted for academic pursuits. I couldn't concentrate very well, she told me, and so my standards were set low. As long as I could tell whose name was on the label of a Christmas present, she was not alarmed.

Dad was also pretty frank. He said I shouldn't be so dumb all the time, but then I couldn't take him very seriously. He also said I had a birdchest, and he called me a number of other things that didn't make sense. Anyway, these names, spoken in a humorless flourish, were only to be taken as endearments. Calling me names was a way of calling me *his*, without having to pat me on the back or touch me. I think in every picture of my early childhood, I am wearing my clothes wrong because he'd dress me in a haphazard way. My pants were pulled up too high, my hat was pulled down over my ears. This was because my father always had this fear of touching me. If he'd show me any affection, it was only to grant me my independence.

My father understood that literacy was important, but

not on the same level as money or reputation. For him, literacy was only a symbol, like getting a politically sensitive joke. By now I should have gotten the joke. I didn't.

For both parents, literacy was only an ambiguous notion. It meant something like having the ability to maintain equal leverage in a conversation, to follow logic, or to use a map to get to some place I'd never been. They could not have imagined how illiteracy could be an average or ordinary part of life. Having not thought through either question at much length, they might have agreed that literacy was natural, and that becoming literate was an inevitable development. They might have thought that someday illiteracy could be eliminated completely, even while they sat and watched television. Literacy was like regular life to them, theirs by sovereignty. They didn't know what to do with me.

Aside from my brother's collection, there were few books in our house. Dad kept a handful of popular novels by the toilet. For this reason, I don't know if he read them. These included works by Tom Clancy, John Grisham, James Clavell, and Gary Jennings, the author of one mammoth work of historical fiction: *Aztec*. It took all of my strength to carry this book in one hand. The cover of the hardback, illustrated with blocks of heavy sandstone, made it look even bigger. I thought of my father like he was Montezuma. I imagined him on the throne, this brick in hand: the symbol of his kingdom.

When news about the presidential election was on we kept our talk to a minimum. Ronald Reagan smiled at us in our living room, his hair lacquered like bowling lanes. Dad viewed the set from his corduroy La-Z-Boy, the footrest up.

Mom wore a nightgown, and smoked a cigarette from her matching recliner. Joe sat on the tweed sofa, a novel on his knee. I lay on my elbows, my back to everyone, my nose a few inches from the static buzzing screen. I blurred my eyes, and lost the crisp images to a grid of micropixels. This was our family tableau, the posture we took when there was nothing left to do.

"Sit back, Travie."

"I can see fine, Mom."

"It's bad for your eyes, Travie."

"It's exercising my eyes, Mom."

"Travis," Father said, sternly.

I crawled back six inches and continued staring. In a few minutes, I got up and filled my glass with water. While resuming my place on the floor, I took those few inches back. There, the set engulfed me like the windshield of a spaceship. I wasn't watching a movie anymore, or hearing the soundtrack; I was seeing light fluctuate in rhythms, unique, random intensities shifting independently in bars of red, blue, and green, like the light show in *Close Encounters of the Third Kind*.

"Travie?"

"What?"

"Sit back."

"I did."

"Son, I can't see through your head."

By eight-thirty or nine o'clock, no one had anything left to say. Dad lumbered off in his boxer shorts, leaving my mom with a glass of Southern Comfort and the remote control.

I slept in the back bedroom, all the way down the hall on

the left. I had a green carpet and wallpaper that consisted of the faces of animals in some far-off wilderness. The bear, the ram, the zebra; their eyes floated out in the middle of the room, heads detached from their bodies. I drifted off to sleep as though lying among them and allowed all the things I had learned that day to return to their simpler and separate natures.

CHAPTER THREE

The Pledge of Allegiance

By the time I began the third grade, Joe and I rode our bikes to school. He had a black Huffy mountain bike with fat tires and straight handlebars. I had a bright red Schwinn Sting-Ray with a glittering gold banana seat. It had coaster brakes, full chrome fenders, chopper handlebars, tassels, and grips that had a groove for each of my fingers. Even on this little bike, I could stand up, pull the bars back and forth, and always outpace my brother.

Backpacks strapped snug to our shoulders, chains around our seats, we cut a little off-road path through our neighbor's backyard and then took a set path through the parking lot of a Baptist church on the corner of 142nd Street. Nine blocks down Garden Drive we made a left and coasted another three blocks. There were other ways we could have gone, other routes we could have taken, but Joe never explored them. He was in charge, and that meant he was only prepared to do as he'd been told.

After the last stop sign, we appeared just east of the playground and pedaled up onto the sidewalk through an opening in the fence. There, Joe and I locked our bicycles behind the cafeteria. Older kids from the safety patrol stood around the intersections wearing orange belts and badges. Children lined up outside the doors, waiting for the bell. Cars and vans and school buses pulled up and drove away again. We separated without talking. His friends were his friends, and we were not friends. In the courtyard, Joe pretended I didn't exist. He wasn't going to be nice to me unless he had to be. He stood with the others in his class, his head high. I joined my friends Bruce, Vance, and Rodrigo under a knotted oak tree. There, before class, we turned up our shirtsleeves like hooligans, exchanged insults, spread rumors, and cracked our knuckles thoughtlessly.

At a quarter after seven, the bell rang across the schoolyard. Then the doors opened and, in hundreds, children rushed inside. My friends walked slowly, in no hurry to be talked down to. At half past the hour, the second bell rang and all the classroom doors were swiftly shut by their teachers. The room went still, except for me—my knee bouncing. I was eager to run back outside. I disliked the building and the small rooms; beige walls, smudged murals, old desk chairs. There were no lockers in the hallways, only classroom doors decorated with construction paper and crayon. The whole cafeteria, the stage and auditorium, were below an expanse of the I-95 expressway. When we ate lunch, our tables grumbled from the passing traffic. The windows were barred and darkened. The plastic knobs on the faucets were worn faceless. Walking down the hall, I felt like I was in some sort of engine built for the purpose of organizing memories.

I wore a striped shirt and tucked my hair behind my ears. Like every other kid in third grade, I brought my lunch in a box and sat down at a gray metal desk. I was given an assigned seat, one aisle from tall fiberglass windows. As the speakers crackled, Mrs. Helene stood before the classroom facing the American flag. The class stood for "The Star-Spangled Banner," which we sang beneath our breath in all variety of sighs, moans, and satires: *"José can you? Sí . . ."* Then we gave a woeful recitation of the Pledge of Allegiance, closing in unison with "and justice for all." The word *justice* came unthinkingly out of our mouths like old bottles in new pop machines.

Each day unfolded in a routine way. We began with our social studies books. The second hour we moved on to our math books. Mrs. Helene led us, adding and subtracting numbers on the chalkboard. At the start of the third hour, she asked us to pass up our "vocabulary exercises." I froze. *What* exercises? We weren't *exercising*. Then the whole room of students did a familiar dance in their chairs, turning and reaching into their backpacks. I copied their movements, rifling through one of the two empty folders in my bag. As my neighbors began to pass up their vocabulary words, I lowered my head and handed up nothing. The next day the same thing happened, and with no consequence.

I learned to pull a blank sheet of paper from my folder and wait. When my neighbor's homework was being passed up, I included the blank, adding it to the bottom of the pile. Then, as though performing a card trick, I would pass the stack forward, leaving the last page—the decoy—spinning on my desk. To anyone in the front of the classroom, it would seem I had turned something in. I became so accustomed to this shuffling technique that I began to grow concerned. If I did turn in homework, any homework, Mrs. Helene would only come to expect more from me.

The part I hated most was the chanting. Mrs. Helene would call out the first word from a vocabulary list, and the classroom would respond by spelling out each word.

"*Walk,*" she began.

"W, A, L, K."

Together, the cacophony of disconnected sounds made my temples whirl. Mrs. Helene asked us all to speak up. "You can be as loud as you want to be," she said with a wink. She wanted us to be heard all the way down the hall, breaking these words into pieces. I pretended to spell out the words, making up sounds as I went along. I tried to listen, but I found that I couldn't chant while I listened, so I chose to ignore the words themselves and say, under my breath, anything I felt like saying.

When Mrs. Helene gave us the next word, voices came up around me again:

"*House.*"

"H, O, U, S, E."

"*House.* Very good, now *purse.*"

"P, U, R, S, E."

"*Purse*. Very good, now *road*."

"R, O, A, D."

"*Road*. Very good, now *bridge*."

As the chanting continued, I found the empty volume of consonants disorienting. I didn't know what I was hearing. I lowered my head, and spent the hour hiding behind other students, who themselves were hiding behind students, all of us hiding from Mrs. Helene.

"*Train*."

"T, R, A, I, N."

One morning Mrs. Helene stepped away from the front of the class and walked down the aisle, looking over each student's shoulder. Soon she was at my side.

"Travis, what page are we on?"

"Am I on the wrong page?"

"You haven't been paying attention," she said, announcing my confusion to everyone.

"I've been trying, Mrs. Helene. I promise."

"How can you say that? You're not reading with the rest of class. Are you?"

"I must have lost track."

"Thirty pages ago!"

I started flipping forward, but then Mrs. Helene reached between the pages of my workbook. Her rings and bracelets scared my hands away. She turned to page 52 and smoothed the sheets down.

I tried to imagine some connection between the workbook and the vocabulary exercises she was always asking of us. She shook her head. "You're not trying. That's why you're on the wrong page." It must have seemed like I was coming out of a spell. "Does your mother know that you haven't been doing your homework?"

I said nothing.

"Do you know what you are supposed to be doing in your workbook?"

I looked back with only the image of a blank piece of paper in my eye.

"I'm going to have to call your mother. Is that okay?"

"You won't find her," I said, impetuously.

"Oh? And why is that?"

"She isn't home."

"No? Where is she?"

"She gets home late." This was the truth. My mother was taking night classes.

"What about your father? Does he get home late too?"

"No, but he doesn't answer the telephone."

"I'll find your parents." I looked down at page 52 until she walked away.

As usual, I rode home with my brother that day. We didn't talk, and I didn't tell him what Mrs. Helene had told me. When my mom and dad came home, I didn't tell them either. I thought I shouldn't tell anyone what happened. If I could intercept the message from Mrs. Helene, no one would have to know about my trouble in school. The event would go unnoticed. Mrs. Helene would have to believe that I was telling the truth. My parents were unavailable. What else could she believe? I imagined how the whole event could fit inside of this single secret and disappear without a trace of wrongdoing. My parents would never suspect. I would only have to answer the phone and be diligent about checking the mailbox.

How long was third grade anyway? Given the heat in Miami, I imagined one day must seem so like the next that the sameness of days would sometimes melt into one sweltering blur, allowing for small changes like this to disappear into the background as though they'd never occurred.

Still, I would check. I had to know for myself. After school, every day for about a week, I screened the answering machine and checked the mailbox, grateful that I wasn't in trouble yet. Then, after a Boy Scout meeting, I found a thick envelope in the mailbox addressed to "The parents of Travis Culley." A few printed letters on the return address confirmed my fear. This had been sent from "Dade County Public Schools," the seal of authority. I shook it. The envelope was full, the lip bulging.

I became unsure if I should still enact my plan. I worried that I could be in some danger if I did not find out exactly what was in this envelope.

This fear came with two realizations: first, that if I was ever to be understood by anyone, I would have to know what Mrs. Helene had sent; and second, one way or another it would be up to me to be smart enough to pass the third grade. I brought three envelopes and a catalog to the table where the bills were sorted and set them all down. Then I hurried outside into the backyard, climbed the avocado tree, and looked back onto the shadows of our house. There, balancing, I had a third realization: if I was too dumb to read and write, too dumb to be loved, then I would someday have to face it.

Mom called me in that night, envelope in hand. She sat me down at the dining room table and set down a pad of paper for note taking. "How have you been doing in school?" she began.

Oh boy. "I haven't been getting all my homework in."

"Why not?" she asked, her pen raised.

"Too much television?"

"But you're not supposed to watch television unless you have all of your homework done. That is a rule."

"You shouldn't turn it on."

We looked over at my father, watching. Then she handed me the envelope.

I handed it back. "You read it."

Inside, a number of forms were stapled together. The first page had something of a title: "Notice of Intent to Conduct an Evaluation." The letter recommended I go through a screening process to determine whether or not I had a learning disability. Depending on how I did—or didn't do—I could be eligible for a program from the Office of Exceptional Student Education.

I must have appeared exceptional to Mrs. Helene, because she recommended me for testing in each of these categories:

- ☑ Intellectual ability
- ☑ Academic achievement
- ☑ Vision screening or evaluation
- ☑ Hearing screening or evaluation
- ☑ Speech screening or evaluation
- ☐ Language screening or evaluation
- ☑ Social/developmental history

- ☑ Behavior observations
- ☑ Learning abilities
- ☐ Anecdotal records
- ☐ Records from other agencies
- ☐ Other: ____________________

I can't say why Mrs. Helene didn't check the box for "Language screening." The only reason I can imagine is that, in the context of Miami, a language screening might be reserved for students who had come from other countries and needed to learn English.

The date was set, and I awaited it anxiously. That January, on the annual Stanford Achievement Tests, my scores had fallen. I had 27 percent in language, 22 percent in reading comprehension, and 24 percent in math computations. I received a shining 16 percent in science. My highest mark was the 49 percent I'd earned in the concept of numbers.

Mom could see there was a problem. She began to make a space for me beside her at the dining room table when she was studying for her midterm exams. There, for about three or four weeks, we did our homework together. She was working on *sublimation* and *substitution*. I was working on *subtraction*. She checked my answers and said with disappointment: "How did you get this?" I kept quiet. If I said too much, she'd only interrupt me.

One night, seeing that I had gotten nearly every answer wrong on my worksheet, Mom leaned over her psychology textbook and asked me: "What happens?"

"What happens where?"

"What happens when you try to do a problem?"

I said, "I look down at the paper. Numbers come into my head through my eyes. Then they move around inside until I have another number, or a solution. I concentrate on that number. I get my pencil and go to write it down. But that's when something happens. The number disappears, somewhere between my hand and my pencil. Then in a hurry to remember what I saw, I write down whatever comes to mind first."

My mother told this story on every occasion that someone asked about how I was doing in school. With it, she could evade the question. If she could laugh about it, she seemed to be saying, they should laugh about it. Any serious consideration of my literacy was thereby hidden behind a spell of nervous laughter.

CHAPTER FOUR

Super-Vision

Joe called it the "Learning Disability Test," sounding each word out with a cartoon voice. I had to take it more seriously. The thing was, as Mom explained, this would be a diagnostic test. I laughed. The word *diagnostic* made my ears tingle. She said there was no way to study. I could not pass or fail. I could only try to make a good impression. It seemed like a tricky situation. I began to envision myself, looking at myself, hoping to see in a reflection what everyone thought was so dumb about me. I had round eyes, and a polite demeanor. Maybe I smiled too much. I thought about how I answered questions, how I spoke, if I stuttered, or hesitated while speaking. I didn't. In class, I began listening a little more closely when kids spoke up. When the room began chanting, I tried to imagine what I was hearing.

If I ever hoped to be a fourth grader, I would have to convince someone that I understood this material. So, for Mrs. Helene, I began chanting. First, I just made sounds. Sometimes I could correctly guess the first letter or two of a word, but then I would leave the rest to gibberish. I had no idea how letters combined into words. I imagined that it would all make sense eventually. What was the term? *Second nature.*

When the day was over, Mom asked if I had any homework.

"I did it in class already," I said. The next day, I said that none had been assigned. I was not only avoiding homework. I was avoiding the embarrassment that would follow whenever the subject of school came up. I stuck to my answers. Both were new to me, and both were lies. Then, while keeping an eye on other kids, I began to suspect that I could cheat my way through class. Who would know the difference?

I began to ask to look at other kids' homework before the morning bell. The first few looked down and shook their heads. When I came upon my next-door neighbor, Lee Michael, he agreed to help. He opened his folder and knelt down. There, one place in front of me, I saw a clean sheet of paper with twenty vocabulary words written neatly in two columns. I squinted over his shoulder and, in my own folder, copied what I saw. When Mrs. Helene asked for our homework, I passed mine up. The next day we did the whole routine again. I asked my neighbor if we could meet before school until I got caught up, and to my surprise he said yes. He even offered to come over to the house after school and help me complete the homework. Here, I said no thanks. My parents didn't like visitors, but more importantly I realized that if Lee Michael were to help me do my assignments, it would defeat the purpose of my not doing them.

One night, I stole away to my room and set the workbook on the end of my bed. I was going to see if I was as smart as other kids were. I gathered all of my mental powers and looked at the vocabulary pages. I found the daily exercises: twenty sentences, each sentence with a blank line in the middle and a corresponding list of words on the next page. I concentrated, but with each word the sentence meant something different. Words were words. Any one could fit into another position. It all seemed pointless. I tried to imagine these words turning those words into sentences, but it didn't help. I only found broken pieces of sentences with only occasional lines converging.

Frustrated, I turned to the back of the book and found the chapter summaries. All the answers, one through twenty, were listed upside down. I spun the workbook around and copied what I saw. The next morning I turned in my homework without having to bother Lee Michael. He looked confused as I proudly turned my assignment in.

Then, on the night before a test, I developed another method. Referring to the answers, I made a tiny cheat sheet. I grabbed a pair of scissors and cut the words away until I had a two-inch square. I folded that square up into a tiny booklet, and set it in the pocket of my backpack. In class, at the third hour, I reached into my bag for my *exercises* and, amid all of the movement in the room, safely withdrew my cheat sheet. By the time the vocabulary test was handed out,

I had the answers waiting beneath the heel of my left hand. I filled in the answers to the test, taking little pauses and shaking my hand to appear as though I was thinking. The next week, I earned my first official A.

"That wasn't so hard," Mrs. Helene said with a smile in her eyes.

♦ ♦ ♦

On the day of the evaluation, Mom drove me to a gray building by the airport where I was introduced to a severe-looking doctor in a white lab coat. She had short white hair and cold eyes. There was no lobby. The doctor sat me down in a bulky wooden chair and talked to me across a large metal table. She began the test immediately, giving instructions and directions. If I had a question she'd stop, look at me, and repeat her instructions exactly as she had before, never getting more specific, and never clarifying my question.

I was given a set of cards to arrange according to the shapes on them, and another set of cards to arrange into a story. I was given cards with cartoons on them. I had to give each of them an expression that matched what they were doing. The doctor wrote my answers on a score sheet. These games went on. Each came with new instructions that she could not make clearer. I pointed, I answered questions, and I turned cards. Soon the test was over, and the doctor was collecting the materials.

"Do you have any other questions?"

"Why do you wear a lab coat?"

"Well, Travis"—she blinked—"we have to control the elements of the test. I wear a coat so that you won't come to think of me as being one kind of a person or another." I looked at her, I thought she was a jerk, and I left.

The results were not quite what anyone had expected. The doctor said that I was possibly dyslexic, but that I was intellectually equipped to stay in the third grade. I had an IQ of "107, adjusted from a score of 111." I was of above-average intelligence, and mostly needed to work on "sequencing skills." She recommended only that I receive more supervision when doing my homework, and if I did not receive this supervision, further counseling might be necessary.

"Super-vision?" I said, rolling my eyes around in my head. "Am I going to get *super-vision*?"

"That's X-ray vision," my brother said, dully.

That night, we sat around the faux wooden box like a family of doves cooing. There would be no seeing through walls, and yet, to my mother's dismay, there would also be no specific name to call my trouble by.

I kept forging my way through Mrs. Helene's class, improving my methods every week. No one had to know how I was getting work in. Mrs. Helene didn't seem to care. She was looking for results only, and results were shallow. She was not concerned with comprehension or understanding, and who was? I began to wonder, if adults were so smart, why didn't I ever hear them explaining things—even to each other?

Had anyone asked me at this time how it was that I learned, I would have told them: *I learned from the kid nearest me.*

About a month before the end of the year, Mrs. Helene's assistant took me aside during the second hour and quietly told me that I might have a tracking problem. To see for herself, she had me try a new approach to my last math quiz. On it, I saw a number of red Xs on four rows of problems.

"Let's have you try these again."

"Again?"

"Go ahead. Erase a wrong answer, and try to correct it."

I erased, tapped my pencil, and wrote down a new answer. She shook her head.

"Okay, we're going to try something." The assistant then took a blank piece of paper out of her desk drawer and pinched the middle of the page. Then, with a small pair of scissors, she cut four small lines in the middle, carefully extracting a one-inch square. Through this square, she said, I should try seeing only one problem at a time. I set that paper down and found the numbers waiting all alone as though in a window. Holding down this cover sheet, I erased the wrong numbers, tapped my pencil, and answered the next problem correctly. I spent the rest of the hour with the assistant quietly correcting problems. The assistant gave me a congratulatory smile when I was done, and I went back to my chair feeling as though I had finally learned something.

When I told my mom about what had happened in class, she doubted me. She thought there was nothing really brilliant about cutting a hole in a piece of paper. To her, the approach meant something different.

"Travie," she said as she looked down at my worksheet, "how much is seventeen minus three?" I'd been working on these problems all day.

"Fourteen," I said by rote.

"Okay, so what is twenty-two minus sixteen?"

"Six."

Mom lit up. "You know how to do this! What is nineteen minus nine?"

"Nine. Ten?"

"Twenty-seven minus fifteen?"

I envisioned the problem. "Twelve?"

I didn't need the paper at all, she claimed. She thought I could do the problems in my head easier than on my worksheet.

I wasn't convinced. I held the piece of paper between us and spied her through it. This piece of paper could be the answer to any problem, I objected, because any problem could benefit by being made to look like a simpler problem.

CHAPTER FIVE

Penuél

Any act of literacy involves the impulse to capture a thing by its name. This is no simple power. It requires having a sensitivity to signs and words, and the courage to use them in order to hold oneself in the proper perspective to things. With the right names, accountability can be taken. Without the right names, accountability is impossible. Equally, there are obstacles that, when placed in the way of a child's education, can set this sensitivity off track.

The inability to read or write is usually understood to come from some lack of experience, poverty or distance in culture, or some inability of the intellect. For some, illiteracy can stem from emotional or psychological decisions—coping mechanisms—which can serve as temporary resolutions for children who don't know how to express their discomfort with the power of right words. This leads to the development of a sort of mental force field for that child, an intellectual defense system, a scanner that when triggered signals only misrecognition and shuts the child down. Illiteracy can become a recourse for traumatized children. They find that the right names for things are hard to reach, hard to trust. Even the right words seem violated, arbitrary, empty, or untenable. Many children learn to protect themselves from the right names of things. Paradoxical ideas will overwhelm them. Every word becomes a reminder of all that cannot be ruled out.

For others, the terms *literacy* and *illiteracy* are inconvenient because they don't begin to identify the many subtle influences or obstacles that prevent literacy, or block literate development. The terms do not account for pathologies in literacy, or hidden forms of illiteracy, and they do not question the measurements we use or the rules we accept as our standards for literacy. These can be biased. *Literacy* and *illiteracy* lack subtlety. Literate people should find better terms, as there are always deeper distinctions to be found.

Many people think illiteracy is a condition that is never improved on without support and therapy, but that's not true. Some will adopt literacy early, and find no way to look back. Others will find they have good reason to keep their illiteracy intact.

♦ ♦ ♦

On Mother's Day, my mom took the Hippocratic Oath, an ancient agreement made by healthcare practitioners. She called it the "unconditional love" clause. I saw my mother chanting in a line of other graduates. I couldn't understand every word, but when they came to "In every house where I come I will enter only for the good of my patients," my eyes lifted. Mom graduated with her master's degree in social work from Barry University. As she did, I took the posture of complete belief in her, and total acceptance of her authority. I have a photograph from the ceremony. She is in the center of the image, diploma in hand, walking in a long black robe. I am in the foreground wearing her cap, leading something of a victory march through the courtyard. On this day, if I had a flag I would have been waving it for my wonderful mother. I had nothing but pride in her and confidence in my family.

As she crossed the stage and accepted her diploma, the audience looked up. I thought she must really know everything. On the drive home she corrected me. She was now a master of handling a person in crisis—that's how she described it—only that. Still, I thought it considerable. To me it seemed that she worked on an immaterial plane, and was a practitioner of specialized psychological techniques. She did not work with tools. She said she was someone who worked on *background processes,* the kinds of things that are going on when nothing is going on.

She used words like *conscious* and *unconscious. Tools* were usually defenses that *clients* used to keep their background processes from being exposed in an untimely way. Words like *projection* and *denial,* these were some of the defenses she was now a master of.

Dad said, "Good job."

"For what? Walking across the stage?" At this time, I couldn't imagine what she meant. Later, I understood. While my mother had depended on my father to get through school, she felt he didn't respect her choice of study.

"You looked good up there." That's all he said.

She frowned, hiding her thoughts, and smoothed out the fabric of her gown. After two years of study at the dining room table, she was now preparing herself to go out into the working world again. Before this would happen, Dad thought she deserved a little break, like a vacation—but without leaving town, and no kids. Dad decided that he could take a week off of work, and send Joe and me to a remote church camp in the Ocala National Forest that he had gone to when he was a boy. He would then have the whole week to spend with his wife, relaxing.

The moment Dad brought the idea up, I didn't like it. I enjoyed the outdoors but had never spent a night out of the house alone, and neither had I ever been placed under the supervision of a church group. We never went to church. Why spend a week with a congregation of strangers, and be ministered to by pastors or priests we didn't know or have any reason to listen to? It didn't make sense.

Dad assured me that I would enjoy myself when I got there, and besides, he said, "you'll be surrounded by friends."

"My friends are here, Dad."

"You're eight, Trav. Don't forget it. When you're eight, your friends are wherever you are." He said church camp was the home of the happiest memories of his childhood. In a lilting voice, he told us about how for one week of every year he and his older brother would be given free rein on the lake and in the forest. When I still looked doubtful, he said sharply: "Listen, if it was good enough for your father, it'll be good enough for you." Then he turned on the television.

Before we left for Daytona, we went down a list of items to pack. It included things like clothes for seven days, a swimsuit, a towel, a pillowcase, an extra pair of sneakers, sunscreen, bug spray, and soap. At the bottom of the list was "shaving cream."

I looked at my father. "What do we need shaving cream for?" Joe and I were both many years from needing to shave.

"We'll get you your shaving cream."

"Do I need a razor?"

Dad tapped me on the back and told me I would understand when I got there.

After loading the car, we pulled out of the driveway and began a long drive northbound on the turnpike. We spent one night at our grandmother's house and got up early to watch the sunrise with my grandfather on the beach.

At about ten in the morning Joe and I were let out of the car in a church parking lot. Kids were being loaded into school buses. Dad boarded with us and started to load our stuffed pillowcases into the overhead carrier. Mom snapped photographs, waving.

The moment we sat down, the whole bus was given a big southern welcome by a gleaming preacher. He prayed for us. Then, on command, the bus drove out onto the street. Children were waving out of the windows until there was nothing, only a road, a bus full of strangers, and my brother sitting next to me, *reading*.

The drive was about an hour long. We passed through a few small towns, and then we followed a dirt road into the woods. After a few bumps and turns we pulled into a clearing with a swimming pool, a baseball diamond, and a small cluster of red barns. When we got off the bus I could see there was a lake and beyond that, for thirty miles it seemed, nothing but kids and trees.

The camp had been a farm before. Dad's church bought the land and made renovations, converting the barns into a mess hall and cabins for the boys and girls. Then they added a swimming pool. Dad said that he had learned to swim at this camp when he was our age, "everyone did." Later they built a chapel, a wide building with a stone fireplace against the back wall and a plywood stage. Construction was still fresh when my brother and I sat down in the pews.

At camp, ritual and tradition determined every minute. A bell rang to start the day. Breakfast was served in the mess hall. After prayers and announcements, we were assigned chores. Some days it would be my job to wash dishes. Some days it would be my job to clean the canoes. Some days I was asked to sweep the boys' cabin and to put the dust into a trashcan that another boy would take out.

Every summer, campers freely and liberally wrote their names on the interior walls of the cabins where we slept. There was no rule that you could not, so everyone did. Most kids marked a place near the bunk of their choice, to claim it as theirs. BILL SLEPT HERE, 1971. ANDREW, 1968. While sweeping, I had a rare chance to be in the cabin alone and to look at all of the kids' graffiti. Names were written over names. Writing went everywhere, overlapping itself. Signatures scarred the wooden windowpanes, the ends of the bedposts, the beams and joists in the ceiling. Writing covered every wall, inch by inch, panel by panel, rising up the sides. With each summer, the barn collected more names.

After doing our chores, kids broke up into two groups for classes. The schedule went as follows: swimming classes were mandatory—even if you knew how to swim. If you took swimming in the morning you took Bible study in the afternoon; if you took swimming in the afternoon, then you had craft making in the morning. Joe and I chose the craft making option because I didn't read, and because he did not believe in God.

The day began in the chapel with a small group of kids. Joe and I spent a few hours mixing watercolors and painting plaster statues. After peanut butter sandwiches and pop, we changed into our swim shorts and leapt into the pool.

In the afternoons, after swimming, a volunteer would start up the boat and take kids around the lake on inner tubes or water skis. At night, after dinner, there were a variety of scheduled events. Tuesday night, we played Capture the Flag on the baseball field. Wednesday night there were board games in the mess hall. Thursday night was a talent show, and on Friday night we sat around a bonfire and listened to the older campers tell scary stories about a deranged lunatic who lived in the woods across the lake and preyed on innocent campers every summer.

When it was time for bed, the adults put out the fire and sent us up the hill from the fire pit. The boys and girls separated into two groups, walking up to our respective cabins to say our prayers with one of the youth ministers. They turned out the lights.

♦ ♦ ♦

On the last night of camp, after dinner and an evening prayer, a special service was held in the chapel. I remember the sound of children clomping through the doorways and around the pews. Behind the preacher, a guy with a mustache playing a guitar led the group in songs. Children sang along, reading from a book of hymns. I sat down near the back of the congregation, a leafy book open in my lap, trying to follow the tabs. Joe sat next to me. The guitarist played, the children sang.

Then the preacher became solemn. He began telling us about original sin, Adam and Eve, naming the animals. Song after song, the preacher became more serious. He approached the pews telling the story of Noah, and the fall of Sodom and Gomorrah. He told us about Jacob wrestling with the stranger by the bank of a river:

"Jacob and the man fought all night, and with every blow Jacob made he took a blow of equal power, and so the fight lasted all night, until the morning light could be seen. When morning came, Jacob asked the stranger what his name was, but the stranger would not give it."

Again the guitarist began to play, and the preacher turned to the hymnbook. We were being invited: "Will you accept Jesus Christ into your heart to be your Lord and Savior?" One by one, children stood from the pews. "Now is your chance," he urged, drawing us onto the stage. First there was one, then there were three, and then there were five more.

"What is your name?"

"William."

"And do you accept the good Lord to be your Savior, William?"

"I do."

"Say it with me: I accept the Lord Jesus Christ. . . ."

"I accept the Lord Jesus Christ. . . ."

"Your new name is Michael, William Michael, and the good Lord will look after you all of your days, and will reserve a place for you in heaven, William Michael." William Michael joined the others onstage. "And you?" He beckoned from the altar. "Are you going to accept God's invitation?" Rob was now Mark. Children who already had biblical names were given second names. James was given Matthew. Andrew was given Paul.

Language, the preacher's power to name and rename children, was like a tool in his hand, a branding iron he waved before us. I looked to my brother. Was he going to go up there? Would he accept a different name? Something held me in my seat. The tool didn't work on me. I pulled the edge of my brother's shirt and sat on it so that he would not budge. I was the illiterate one, I would protect him.

As the pews thinned out, the stage grew crowded with children. I thought about the names in the cabin, and I understood what the camp was for. Camp was a system of experiences built to separate us from our parents.

Once all of the other congregants had gone up, the red-faced man looked out at Joe and me, sitting shoulder to shoulder. His head shining, the preacher urged us to accept the Savior and to follow the others. Veins pulsed behind his ears. We did not stand. We did not understand. Bereft, the preacher gave a closing prayer.

After the service, all of the children were called to the mess hall for the end-of-the-week party. It was Carnival Night. There were decorations and refreshments. The adults had set up tables with a different game on each. At one table there was a dart-throwing game, at another an apple-bobbing contest. There was a game of Twister, a basketball hoop, and, near the bathrooms, a big heart-shaped kissing booth with red curtains.

In front of the booth, boys and girls waited in line. It amused me, the red drapery and the heart-shaped frame. There was even a mirror in the entranceway, where kids brushed their hair and puckered their lips. Never before had I been witness to a true kissing booth. Interested, I stepped in line behind the others. I had never kissed a girl before, and wasn't sure what to expect. When I considered that I didn't know *who* I might be kissing, I thought about stepping back out of line. It may not have been the right time to do this.

Then, from across the room, one of the adults noticed me. Before I knew it, he was beside me, holding my arm tight. In a low voice he told me I shouldn't be in this line. I was too small, he said. Then he sat me down at one of the wooden picnic tables. "Now, just wait here. I've got something for you." He stood, and walked to the kitchen.

I waited. Kids were going into the kissing booth and

slowly, one after the next, coming out the other end. I looked down at my ankles, crossed beneath me. The man returned with a red cup. He didn't know my name, but he talked to me through his mustache as though he did know my name. "I got you some pop," he said. "You thirsty? Drink this up, okay? This is for you, okay? Don't share it with anyone else." He nodded as he spoke.

Holding the plastic cup in both hands, I couldn't figure out the flavor. It tasted like ginger ale, but it was darker than ginger ale, and sweeter. The man was satisfied with me when I sipped from it. I wasn't in trouble anymore. Then he left me on the bench with my drink. In the back of the mess hall, I saw a girl looking over at me, and I thought she might have seen what had just happened. Without thinking much, I walked over and introduced myself. She said her name was Angela.

"Did you see that?" I asked. "That man just pulled me out of line."

"What for?"

"He said I was too small to go into the kissing booth."

"You're not too small."

I was flattered, yet cautious. I sipped from my cup and asked her if she had been in.

"In where?"

"In the kissing booth?"

Angela looked away. She wasn't planning on going in either. I wondered what was inside. Was there a boy and a girl in there? It would only seem right. Was there a countertop, or a table that they leaned over? Who were the lucky volunteers who had been chosen to kiss the kids at camp? It had suddenly become too loud at the carnival. Angela couldn't hear me.

Sipping from the dark ale, I invited her to go outside so that we could hear each other better. She agreed, and I held open the screen door. We walked past the vending machines with the pop drinks in those old glass bottles. I remembered the satisfaction of wrenching the caps from them for fifty cents, and I remembered the taste of a cold caramel honeycomb on my tongue. This was different. I sipped from a flat sour cup and followed Angela into the beam of a spotlight that was mounted to the roof of the old barn. The light was too bright. We squinted, and walked down the hill to the empty swing set glowing in a pool of moonlight.

Angela sat in the seat of one swing. I put my cup down in the sand, and asked her if she wanted a push. She said she was afraid of heights. I wasn't afraid. I loved heights and so I took the swing next to her and started kicking myself into the air. Maybe Angela would push me.

"Just wait. I'll go all the way up!" I said.

My head was spinning. It had become a beautiful night with a clear, full moon that hung over the lake. I felt a tingle of deep excitement I had no name for. I felt I could hold the moon in one hand. On the swing, I experienced something of a miracle. It seemed there were two moons. One was hung from the night looking down, and the other was the first moon's reflection wading in the glassy lake, looking up. As I swung, the distance between the two moons appeared to lengthen and shorten. Angela watched me from below. I was lifted up so high that the chains went loose in my hands. I held on until gravity came and snapped them taut again. Then I decided to jump from the swing. I thought I would land on my feet in the grass below.

"Watch this!" I cried, making my last few kicks. Eager to fly, I turned my wrists under and threw myself into the space between two moons. Hearing the chains ring above me, I lost all perception of the ground. I fell hard, knocking myself out on the packed earth.

I awoke to find the man with the mustache telling Angela to go inside. She ran up to the light. I had dirt in my mouth. I brushed pebbles away from my face. The man with the mustache picked me up in his arms as though I were a guitar and carried me down the hill and toward the lake. I kicked out of his arms, refusing to be carried. I wanted to walk on my own. I was a big boy, I said. The man told me I could walk beside him if we held hands. Feeling dizzy, I let him lead me alongside the pool, and down behind a big tree near the lake. We walked along the bank and then up the other side of the pool, avoiding the light from the mess hall. He walked me to the door of a small white building above the chapel. I was confused. The man had said he was taking me to the clinic, but the door read OFFICE. That much I could read.

The man with the mustache knocked on the door. An older man, expecting us, opened it and whisked me inside. No words were said. Was this the same preacher from the sermon? I couldn't tell. His face was not red anymore, but his eyes were the same glassy blue. The man with the mustache left. The door was closed. The older man went over to the letter-writing desk and began to ask me what happened.

I told him: I'd fallen.

"Swinging too high?"

I repeated my words, knowing what I'd done.

He said he'd give me something for the pain. He was putting on a latex glove, just one, on his left hand. He had a small clear jar and a gauze pad that he drew from the drawer of his desk. He opened the container and poured some of its liquid into the cotton. Gently, he came closer and asked me to show him where it hurt. I lifted up my shirt, over my left side—and then I disappeared, falling right through my skin, feeling the pastor's plastic thumb against my cheek.

One moon had been cut from the night. I woke, spinning, feeling held by the sound of crickets. I was in the anxious embrace of a man, someone. He was bumping me. I had no idea how I'd gotten here, or where I was. I couldn't feel anything but for a sort of glowing in me, and all around me. I could see through my skin. I was aware of my back and legs, my hands and face, even with my eyes closed. Someone was bumping me, and the table I was lying on. I had been dreaming of being in heaven, knowing what heaven was—except for the crickets. I remember thinking there would be no crickets in heaven. God would not bother to populate the clouds with them. I must be on earth. I was in a small room, on a white metal table, beside a piano that was covered with a thin quilt. There were golden crosses on the walls. He didn't think we were in heaven, did he? I felt like I was having an argument with myself, like wrestling with myself. I thought: *If I could just explain, then I would wake up, or he would wake up—or wake himself up.* I placed my arms on the tabletop, and turned to explain about the crickets.

The man stepped back, his collar loose. He collected the tails of his shirt and stuffed them into his pants, adjusting a belt buckle. He was wearing a white shirt and black pants. I sat up and found that my shorts were around my ankles. I was dizzy. I was sick. He said, "You're okay. You're okay. See? No bruises or scrapes." I had no way of understanding what he meant.

Sitting up on the table, I drew my swim shorts up to my hips, and I looked up at the man who had been bumping me. He was old. His cheeks were flushed. He had starch-white hair.

Reaching with my toes, I found the floor, but it was moving. With both feet on the ground I could ask, "Do I have to be here?"

"You don't have to stay here"—he sat back down in the corner—"but you can stay, if you want to." Turning my eyes away from the old man, I walked through the front door, stepping unsteadily down to earth.

He came to the door again and closed it gently, saying only: "Go back to your cabin now. You'll forget everything in the morning."

Outside was infinite night, and I was dizzy. I didn't even know what direction I should walk in until I saw a light over the mess hall, stretching across my forehead in rays. I was at camp, and I was thirsty.

I walked uneasily up to the doors of the mess hall and peered in. The space had been emptied. The carnival had ended. In the mess hall a clock read absolute midnight. Two arrows had collapsed into one and were pointing to a pinhole, the moon, now above me. *Where had this time gone? Where had the children gone?* Then I saw the narrow sidewalk that led back to the cabins. As my eyes adjusted I saw the swing set. There in the sand, a red plastic cup. *Did I leave it?* In the cup, half full of something dark, I saw purple poison. A cold sweat touched my forehead, and I steadied myself. Then I heard a voice. It came from within me:

> *In case something happens, you're going to need to remember this.*

A breeze passed over the lake, drawing fog. Two hours had vanished, maybe more. I saw trees in silhouette. I remembered the lunatic in the woods, and I walked back to the boys' cabin. Opening the screen door, I managed my way down the dark hall between the bunk beds. I recognized my bed by the graffiti on the bedposts. I pulled myself up and fell into my sheets. I laid my head on the pillow, trying to stop spinning. To help myself sleep, I curled up and listened to the sound of the other boys breathing.

As dawn approached, I found the letters of the alphabet moving beyond my reach. Day was here. There was my body; I saw it. I kept floating over, sweeping past it, unsure if this was the body to which I'd been assigned. The names were moving like liquid around the beams and panels of the cabin. The scratches of so many pens and pocketknives cast tiny multicolored shadows into the grain. Colors converged; it wasn't light. Blue ink read green. Red ink read black. Black markers shone orange and yellow.

I heard laughter where children stood to write their names. I saw their markers in hand, tops careening to the floor. I saw all of this clearly, even from my bed, but then it struck me as odd, very odd, the silence. The breathing had stopped. I sat up and leaned over the rail. I was alone in the cabin. All of the other boys had packed their bags and left them on their naked mattresses. I heard laughter. My stomach ached. I had to find the bathroom.

Uneasily, I climbed down from the bunk bed. I was still dizzy. In a stupor, I walked down the hall. Behind me, tendrils of sunlight were moving; names followed me around corners. I pulled down my swim trunks, which I was still wearing. There, I felt suddenly displaced, as though I had never been in this place before. I didn't recognize the little red stall that I was seated in. The toilet and the door were so close together that there was no room to place my knees. I tried to close the door, which wasn't really a door but a board, a piece of siding, hung from a hinge and painted red. As it wafted open with the breeze, I heard the laughter again. The boys and girls were out on the baseball diamond, playing in shaving cream. I saw a stripe of black blood in my hand, and I disposed of it like a bug, flushing. I swore I must have been dreaming. Lines of colored light pierced me. Names seemed to change, trading letters back and forth behind me. I climbed back up into the bunk, pulled my sheets over my head, and thought I should just try to wake up again. *It'll stop,* I assured myself. Above me, everywhere, the seconds whirled forward and back. Hours spun in place. Decades found themselves knotted to the woodwork. ROBERT 1959, STEVE WAS HERE '72, HERB WAS HERE, GERALD '67, MARK '81, NICK SLEPT HERE '75. Years flashed. Gleaming children ran past the windows in swimsuits, their bodies covered in white soap. The lake awaited them. I lay back feeling as though I'd been fighting all night.

CHAPTER SIX

Survival Stories

Stories like mine can be hard to tell. They are often told more easily in a whisper than in full voice, and the reason is plain: a survival story is nothing to celebrate. The right words are hard to find. Even if survivors do succeed in finding them, the most concerned reader will dread reading what they write down. This is why survival stories, truly lived, appear awkward and unfitting in their adaptations, as comedies or tragedies. They tend to have no easy place among the amber and blue hues of the theater. Too often the telling gets in the way. The issues are too delicate. The moral, which is cautionary, becomes too easily cluttered by the conventions of the art. The consequences of any misunderstanding can be far-reaching. There is no room for spectacle, no room for easy resolutions. The hero in a survival story doesn't feel like a hero, doesn't know he is a hero, and the villain can't be taken seriously in costume.

Every day it seems I read another story about victims of the church coming forward. We hear the awful truth about children who have been harmed. Some children are, and when they are it can be a shameful thing to place a name on. Terms can be abused. They can serve as a tool of religion, a branding, a scar. A child who is strong enough to resist a branding deserves to be listened to.

I have to be grateful that the hardships I did experience would not impede my ability to become literate finally, and I have to be most grateful that a process rooted in art would help me to discover and explain all that had stood in the way. Without literacy, without art, without having some process with which to look over the passage of time, I think my grief would have consumed me, and I would never have come to know the full vindication that I have been able to receive by writing. To come this far, I would still have to take a long journey. I would be led even further away from reading. I would have to avoid letters and literacy completely because of what, for a time, I feared they might reveal. I never knew that a boy could be treated the way that I had been, and it was something I did not want to learn.

♦ ♦ ♦

All that I could hope for was a little normalcy. But when Mom emptied our clothes onto the pool table, one heavy tin of shaving cream with red and white stripes fell out onto a pile of jeans and towels. I caught the can as it rolled, and ran it to my room directly. Without thinking, I stuffed the can away in the bottom drawer of the unused desk in my room. Closing this drawer, I knew that I had become a boy with secrets.

School started at the end of the summer, and I didn't want to be there. I sat in a different classroom, looked at my fourth-grade teacher, Mrs. Southard, and decided to forget everything, just as the man had said.

In the coming weeks, I found that I could say I did not know the answer to a question, even when I did. I didn't want my teacher to sense what I had become aware of. I didn't want her to know what was on my mind. I wouldn't think. Why think? Instead, I stepped aside and imagined other possibilities. I refused any attempt at reading or writing—and my rejection was final and radical: I would no longer be the boy I'd been. I would forget myself. See with new eyes. I aimed at forgetting everything that I had learned before this summer, even the images of words I knew, every trace of internal representation. I tried to *not* recognize names, even street signs, no matter how common they were. I de-inscribed them, reversing the letters, scrambling the suffixes and pulling syllables back into misrecognition. I began using the wrong words for things. I said *his* when I meant *hers*, *up* when I meant *down*. My parents thought I was being glib. It seemed to them that I had returned from camp exactly as I'd left.

Knowing that Mrs. Southard would never suspect, I began to play a little game, like Stone-Face, where two people look at each other until someone breaks into laughter. The difference was only that I never told her what I was doing, and she never caught on. I called the game Never-Mind, and the idea was to pretend that I was listening. This way, she would go on and on into exasperation and I would catch no part of the lesson.

In the first few weeks of class, instead of paying attention, I was either scratching mosquito bites on my ankles or drawing tormented action figures on sheets of lined paper. If I couldn't draw because Mrs. Southard had strictly prohibited it, then I began invisibly drawing: flying an airplane far outside of the room, chasing lint off into wholly new dimensions, navigating the ravine of a crinkled page. Then the bell would ring and my mind would come back to me. It was time for recess, and I was one of the other kids again.

This year, Joe had said that he didn't want to ride his bike to school anymore. He said the ride in the morning made him sweaty all day. Dad understood. Soon, a new ritual had been established. In the morning, Joe, a spitting image of his father, climbed into Dad's company car and was whisked away to school.

I pulled my old Sting-Ray out of the carport and rode. Pedaling through the damp morning air, I felt vindicated. I could now take any path I chose. Each morning, this became my whole objective: *How can I take a new route to school?* I didn't want to be followed. I wanted to disappear from my kitchen door and reappear at my desk like magic. Leaning on one pedal, I thought no one should be able to predict my next move or imagine where I might be going. I cut through the church parking lot using the shortcut through our neighbor's yard. On asphalt, I listened to my chain grind and my seat squeak. I wove crisscross lines in a labyrinth of residential streets. When my mind was free to wander, I sat back and coasted.

Under the trees on Fourth Avenue, I thought about how the sky was only a thin blue net holding the earth together. I imagined that if the birds flew high enough, beneath them the whole planet would seem to rest in this blue net, staying afloat as the ground beneath me spun. I saw myself riding underneath this round world. Every street connected to another. The more I rode my bike, the more my imagination seemed to drift into new horizons. Some of the images became so real they would transfix me. Occasionally, I lost track of which world these pictures were set in, and then I found myself standing in the middle of an intersection, unsure of which way to go. It was as though I had found a special place in the corner of my mind from which I could begin to see and think, and when I thought from that place, I thought anew.

On these rides, I began hearing voices. Something of a conversation was taking place in one room of my inner ear. There it was, continuing on as though in my absence. When I first acknowledged that this was happening, the voices receded. The talking stopped mid-sentence, as if they didn't want to be noticed. I thought they were being shy. As I became more aware of them, I learned to attend to them differently: I tried to eavesdrop on myself. Through one ear I could scan for birds or traffic, and the voices would think I wasn't listening. They seemed to think that most people didn't listen. But I was onto them. I kept them in mind. I would fill my head with music, and melodies that I'd make up to give my voices a second to relax. As long as it seemed my thoughts were elsewhere, my voices would resume talking among themselves, playing bridge or telling stories about their neighbors and people they'd read about in the news, things I could never have come up with on my own.

It never occurred to me that this might be the effect of an early psychotic break of some kind. I felt like it was a gift. It made me curious. Every morning, I was tapping into something new. There was no way to tell what I'd be hearing next. I found that these voices, in groups of four or five, were sometimes strangers to one another. In groups of two or three they were familiar, drawn together by some third element. I experienced no other peripherals, no flashes or wave effects like you see in dream spells on TV. I rode home, trying to imagine that everyone heard voices like I did.

In Mrs. Southard's class, I tried to sit at my desk and play Never-Mind, but I couldn't sit still. My name was being called, but no one was calling it. Sometimes I would get confused because I would see the thoughts of my classmates going right across their faces. Much of my time in class I spent wondering how it was that I was even sitting there. Mrs. Southard couldn't tell that I was off in other worlds. I wore a gentle smile and allowed her voice and those I was hearing to distract me from each other. My smile became brighter the sooner I lost track of these crisscrossing conversations. Sometimes Mrs. Southard would speak more loudly, I realized in horror, only to disperse her own inner voices. I tried not to absorb them.

One day she announced that we were going to learn cursive. I sat back: *Not me, not ever!* When I looked at a line of cursive, my thoughts spilled across and over, analyzing the handwriting. *Who writes that way?* Tying these elastic words up in my head until they were tangled, I couldn't be sure what I was seeing anymore. I ran my finger along a word, trying to read the letters in their combinations. The letters wound up so that I could not distinguish one from the other—and I didn't try. The script was easy to imagine being only scribble, so unlike my own cross-hatching. I could imitate these shapes with my pen, but I could not get them to fit together in my mind.

Voices emerged, and I entertained them. I wondered whether or not the people in my head knew cursive. They were always talking. Did they write? What did they write with? They argued against the curvy lines I held in hand. There were always other possibilities.

At times, I found myself lost between likenesses, floating past signs as if I were on my bicycle. Suddenly there was no trace of where I was going or how I had gotten there. All memory of the prior moment had gone. One word replaced another, and then, as through a window in my mind, they went no place.

That spring, on the Stanford Achievement Tests, I came up below average in every subject. Language, 39 percent; reading comprehension, 21 percent; math, 19 percent. On my report card, I received four Ds and two Fs. It was such a disaster that no one at home said anything about it. My grades were only *symptomatic,* my mother said. Of what, she could not say.

CHAPTER SEVEN

Rebel, Rebel

It was like a mask. At Biscayne Gardens I appeared to most people a clear-eyed, jovial child, but in fact I was a different person. I became shy in the presence of authorities. I turned red under observation. I felt punished in myself, in having to be myself. When class was over, I went through a reversal. I became talkative and social. I was ready to play. I was an element of everybody. I thought about intelligence abstractly. I thought that the skill a person must have to translate a sound into a word was based on the adoption of something deeper. I thought maybe this was one of the background processes my mother had talked about.

Of course, I did not know the limits of my own intelligence, nor could I sense its levels. I could not tell—myself—whether or not I was equipped with a high degree of intelligence, a good or bad intelligence, a fast or a slow intelligence. How does one know these things? In my family, it seemed that intelligence did not work like nature worked. Intelligence borrowed and rearranged. Intelligence assumed itself superior, advantaging itself over unthinking things. My brother's intelligence was his advantage over me, in this sense. From his point of view, I was unformed, gentle and dumb. I was the gullible stuff of human nature. I went into the backyard, disappeared behind the cover of trees to discover my own strengths and weaknesses. I was no Birdbrain. I became something of a wild child, Nature Boy, and I hoped to embrace what I did not know. I didn't need to be smart, I needed to be brave and patient.

We had exotic trees, many of which gave fruit. There were paper trees that lined the yard and schefflera at the corners of the house. We had an avocado tree that shook little green pears all over. The mango with its thick snakeskin branches would turn red and drop fruits the size of water balloons. We had an orange tree and four banana trees that bloomed constantly, but we were living on the property like campers in an RV. We camped in the house. Dad camped in his chair. Every weekend, Dad had Joe and me stand around with rakes and garbage bags, hauling sticks and leaves to the mulch pit by the fence. We ignored the fruit that fell. "They're in our yard," Dad said. "They're dirty." I would turn the unused orbs into little grenades. I stuffed them with M-80s and Black Cats and sent them blasting through the yard at night. On Saturday morning, Dad mowed it all under his tractor, fresh, rotten, or charred. The four-wheeled lawn mower spit avocado seeds out with a pop, and sent mango peels flying. The house was equally ignored. It had been built of brick in the 1930s; we moved in and never touched a thing. We let the hedges grow, and watched the yellow walls fade to powder. The front of the house was hidden by a ficus that was suffocating in vines. From the street, the only signs of real life were our cars, a covered boat in the carport, and our mailbox—its little red flag folded obediently downward.

One day, while playing alone, I heard the laughter of two girls in the neighboring yard. They were in a little wooden house, built between two tree branches. "I see you!" I called. The girls fell quiet. They could not see me, and so I made my way over, barefoot, to a patch of dirt between our yards. I asked if I could come up and see their tree house.

"Boys aren't allowed," the younger girl shouted down.

"Why not?" I asked, too young to understand.

"Because, those are the rules," the older sister added.

"Can I climb your other trees?"

There was a brief pause. "Maybe."

Then, the younger voice: "Not this one!"

I began walking along the top of the stone fence between our yards, boasting about how I could climb any tree, anything at all. The two sisters came down. Dana, the younger, had freckled cheeks and wore ponytails. Melanie was a delicate brunette, my age, with long hair and a perfect smile—but there was something else: she was wearing one green and one white shoe, striped pants, a yellow shirt, a blue denim jean jacket, and a teal bandanna wrapped around her arm. I wanted to make a joke, but she was keeping too careful an eye on me.

"Pick any tree. I bet I can climb it," I said, gazing at all the trees in her yard. She picked an oak tree some twenty feet away.

Pointing, she said: "Okay, there's one."

I ran to the foot of a tree that was twice as wide as the telephone pole that stood between our yards. There were no branches that I could reach with a leap. There were no knots in the trunk. I didn't even know where to begin.

Melanie looked at me with a smile, her hand on her hip. She must have thought this was fun. After hugging the tree for a handful of seconds, I let go. My struggle made Melanie laugh at me. I stepped away, shaking my fingers out. That's how my first childhood crush began. I had found someone as smart as I was daring. For a moment we were aware of our equality. Then I ran over to the fence, and back to my yard, to show her how high I could climb in one of my own trees.

She followed me to the fence but did not cross it. Dana stayed back too, and so I was stuck there again on that stone fence, balancing. Then I realized that I could reach the telephone cables suspended down the length of our yards. At the back corner of our lot there was one of the ubiquitous wooden poles that carried the weight of these black cables as they led from house to house. Dana told me not to, but I did it. I grabbed hold of the electrical cable and hung. The rubber housing was as thick as my grip. I swung, asking Melanie to join me when Dana ran inside. Soon, Mr. Ortiz came out to see what was happening. When he saw me standing about with his daughter, the telephone cable hanging down between our yards, he knew what had happened. I could have killed his daughter.

Mr. Ortiz remained calm as he said, "Don't you ever do that again!" I heard him. It was a true reprimand. He didn't raise his arm like my father did, and I didn't fear that he would hit me. Then he told his daughters to go inside. He said I needed to go back home too—to think about this. I did exactly that. I crept home, listening to all the voices in my head while my newly unemployed father lay facedown on the carpet, asking me to scratch his back.

In a few weeks, the event at the Ortiz house had been forgotten, and I was again allowed over to meet the girls. Mary Anne, their mother, opened the front door when I rang the bell. She introduced me to Melanie and Dana as if it were the first time. Soon I was coming over every day, eager to play. They were happy children, and I was desperate to absorb some of their energy. It was in their timing, in the way they allowed each other to talk, in the way they heard each other through. It wasn't dumb, it was serious.

I told Melanie the recent news at our house. It just came out. "Joe just got into Norland. Do you know about Norland?"

"The gifted school?"

Dade County Public Schools had a handful of magnet schools where kids could apply and receive specialized training in one field or another. Norland was one such school, offering an arts-based curriculum of music, dance, art, and theater to middle school kids. Joe had just been accepted into the visual arts department. My parents were so proud of him, saying he was going to be an artist someday, and buying him all sorts of supplies. I think I brought this up with Melanie to see if she would ever think of auditioning. She clearly had a few streaks of creativity.

"You can get in too if you try," she said.

"I'm not talented."

"If Joe is talented, you are," Melanie said. I thought about this while we spent the afternoon playing. When I walked back in through the front door of my house, my cheeks pink, and wearing different-colored socks, I found my family seated in the same frozen arrangement I'd left them in: Joe with a book, Dad with a beer, Mom with a cigarette.

My next report card came home with recommendations for summer school attached. Joe laughed at me. Mom showed Dad my scores, and he responded with his usual tact: "You just can't go through life being stupid, son. You're going to turn out like Gil, next door."

"David," my mother cautioned him.

"Well, look: we've got a smart son and a stupid son. If you were smart like your brother, you'd get to go to church camp this summer. *Wouldn't you?* See? So, you're too stupid to go to church camp like the other kids. You've got to stay behind." He cracked peanuts and brushed the shells onto the carpet. "How does that feel? I think you should be ashamed of yourself. But that's just what I think."

I turned up my collar. I was very happy to go to summer school, especially if it meant not having to go back to church camp. In fact, until now, I had never been so happy to be called stupid. I thought: *He has no idea what that word means.*

CHAPTER EIGHT

Where the Sidewalk Ends

The story about our shortcut to school, which I now took alone, may shed some light on my father's disposition. It was a small path that Joe and I were permitted to take through the backyard of the Gunbar residence. Only two people lived in this house: Mrs. Gunbar, who was very old and weak and never went outside, and her son, Gilbert, or Gil, who lived in a converted garage. Gil was also very weak. He didn't have a job. He had no place to go. He lived quietly, although he would sometimes upset my dad by turning on the lawnmower late at night, and mowing his yard with the tractor lights on. Dad didn't think he should call the police. He just huffed and said to my brother: "Gives new meaning to 'Tend your own garden.' "

In the morning, I'd see Gil fixing sprinkler heads, and picking up branches in the yard. With his wiry frame and long hair, he looked something like Mick Jagger. We were told, as kids, to avoid Gilbert Gunbar—the neighborhood drug addict—even though he was gentle enough to allow my brother and me to tear a dirt path directly through his backyard. Gil knew the street out front was dangerous. He said, "Cut through anytime."

Joe and I could not refuse the offer, but still we were told to avoid Gil under all circumstances. We saw that he looked thin, pale, his shirt hanging from bones. My mother said, "Reminds me of someone I know."

As a boy, Gil had gone to the regional public schools. He told me an incredible story about when he was a student at Thomas Jefferson Junior High, one of the worst schools in the area. At the time it wasn't so bad, he said. "But you couldn't keep your hair long!" His laughter had a kind of whooping sound, and it came with a cough.

Gil said he was some kind of a math whiz in the seventh grade. He won competitions in calculus and trigonometry. He broke records. His teachers had never seen anything like Gilbert Gunbar before, but he would not cut his hair. The new vice principal would have been forced to expel Gil from school if he did not follow the rules and get a trim. Gil refused proudly, but then he didn't have any money. One day after school, it sounded like the happiest day in his life, he received a visit from the vice principal, who drove him to a barbershop and paid for the haircut himself. Gil laughed, retelling this. He was still moved by it. I listened as though he had not yet reached the end of his story, but he had.

When I came home late from school that day I foolishly told my mother who I had been talking to. She grew very upset. She said Gil was a complete and utter failure in life, and that I shouldn't waste any time *talking* to him. She was being hard on me about this because she didn't want me to turn out like him. If I never set an objective, if I never developed some aim in life, if I never learned to read, she thought, I would become a hedonist and a freeloader, going from pleasure to pleasure without a moment's caution. "What kind of life is that?"

If she had stopped for a second, stopped lecturing, I would have told her what Gil had told me about his having been a math whiz, earning high marks in calculus. She wouldn't hear it. There were simply a hundred other things I should be doing. My mother's ignorance had me incensed. Where was this coming from? I remembered all those other students looking up to her—as I did—receiving her master's degree, and taking the Hippocratic Oath. I thought she had no business looking down on Gil, or on anyone, this way, but I could not find the words to challenge her authority.

At a certain point in life, Rousseau explains, a child becomes possessed of greater strength than he has wits for. As the body changes, the child becomes equipped with seemingly limitless energy, and this sort of excess forces the young mind to become blind to what it cannot do. I was now on the threshold of this kind of limitless energy, and my mother could see how I felt. I knew that the world was bigger than my little horizon, bound and guarded by the prohibitions I received from her.

Playing with other kids, I could tell: not all families lived like I lived or thought like I thought. Pieces were coming together about how distorted my environment was, and I began to be a little more curious about what other people thought. People come from different places. People must think differently.

What I could not have seen coming was that I would become equally misunderstood if I did not fall into conformity with my mother's values. In the years ahead, she would come to misidentify my struggles just as my teachers had. She would soon come to misconstrue the energy I was developing as a young man, taking my exuberance to be anger, and my malaise to be a sign of suspicion and disloyalty.

♦ ♦ ♦

Fortunately, even in grade school, there were teachers who felt it was their responsibility to identify and nurture students like Gilbert Gunbar—to help them harness their creative or analytic gifts. My mother couldn't keep me from one agent of change: Mrs. Carballo, my sixth-grade music teacher.

Over the years we had come to be acquainted through art projects that she would periodically host. Now we were like pals. In the third grade, she'd directed me in a school play. In the fifth grade, I took second place in a talent contest she held. I performed a break-dancing routine that I'd choreographed in the schoolyard with three other boys. Once I asked her about her name, pronounced "Carbaiyo." She wasn't Hispanic, and yet it seemed she had a Hispanic name. She told me that she'd been married. Her smile was so sweet, I could have cried.

In the sixth grade, ten minutes before the end of class one day, I was making kids laugh. Using my xylophone as a mask, and the keys as long teeth, I became a motley curmudgeon and banged my mallet around at the other kids' instruments. Mrs. Carballo took me aside. I thought I was in trouble, but she laughed. As the school bell rang and the classroom cleared, she asked if I had ever thought of applying to a gifted school. I looked down and thought of what my brother might say.

Mrs. Carballo set her hand down on the desk and said, "I think you may have certain talents that are worth exploring."

"In *music*?"

"No, not in music. How about in acting or theater? You've got a terrific personality, Travis, *when you're not in class*," she said with a smirk. "I think you'd make a very good actor." I watched her carefully. Then she told me that my friend Bruce was auditioning for the program. I loosened up. "You know Bruce. Maybe you can take classes with him?" she suggested.

That afternoon I found my mother at home. I went right up to her and told her that I wanted to audition.

She said, "Maybe you should decide to bring up your grades first."

"But Mrs. Carballo recommended me."

"Who?"

"My music teacher."

"The music teacher . . ." Mom said to herself.

"Does she need your permission?"

"No. She doesn't."

"Do I need your permission?"

"Put your bag down."

When the application materials arrived, my mother helped me complete the forms. We went slowly line by line, and I filled in the blanks, printing the words exactly as she told me to. Norland required only three things: I needed to live in Dade County, I had to expect to graduate the sixth grade, and I had to audition with a one-minute monologue.

"A monologue?" My mother laughed, playing with the word. She called the school to have the meaning of the word clarified. "Really?" she asked through the telephone. "I've never seen it used that way before. It's like a *speech,* Travie." She repeated back the instructions: "He needs a one-minute *speech* from a play. Does it have to be memorized? It does." She said grimly, "Oh, Travie, you're going to need to memorize a speech from a play. How about a poem?" she asked into the telephone. "Can it be a poem? Great."

Mom went into Joe's room and pulled out our one volume of Shel Silverstein's poems. "Find something in here," she told me.

Okay, I thought, *it's time I learned to read a poem.*

On the book jacket was an image of the author sitting barefoot with his guitar. He had deep blazing eyes and a dark stare. Without reading, I saw that every poem inside the book coincided with the illustration nearest to it, and each illustration called for a poem. I followed the words I knew, and then I tracked them in the illustrations. There was the pile of garbage, there were the rats. Taken together, with all of the basic ideas literally depicted, I could seem to read without confusion. At least I could validate the words I knew. The illustrations gave me the clue to do what I was supposed to be doing. Now I saw the words like they were drawings, swooping and knocking around until I heard something. Soon, every page had a surprise in store. The more pages I turned, the better I was able to understand the line of associations I was to follow, and the funnier each poem became. After so many years of refusing books, I now had reason to open one.

In the book, I often had a feeling of vertigo, and sometimes I was confused about how to proceed. But I looked at the pages until I felt like I was only listening to them, hearing the drawings speak. For me, reading wasn't a very leisurely activity. I did not sit on the couch and make faces at the book like my brother did. Time was against me. I had to have something for the audition so I threw myself in, reading out of order, speaking aloud what words I knew and guessing on the others. My mother was curious about my motivation, but she stayed out of the way. She'd never seen anything motivate me toward reading.

One of the poems was about a boy who plugged a lightbulb into the sky. One was about a woman who kept her kids in boxes. One was about a boy who turned into a television set—as though watching it was contagious.

Then there was "Sick," a poem about a girl named Peggy Ann McKay. In the drawing, she looks up warily from her bed sheets to the lines of poetry above and across, on the next page. She says she is too sick to go to school today, but as her list of ailments gets longer, each more implausible than the next, it becomes clear that she is saying whatever she can to stay home.

"Mom, what's this word?" I pointed.

"How do you pronounce it, Travie?"

The word was *'pendix* and I couldn't make sense of it.

"Pelvis!" Mother guessed. "Have you never seen the word *pelvis* before?"

How would I know otherwise? It didn't matter to me that she was wrong. I could now read this poem, and that made it unlike any other thing in the world. I showed it to Melanie, and she said it didn't matter that it was written for a girl. I needed to give it my all, my "everything."

I went to work reading the poem over and over again, using *pelvis* in place of *'pendix* every time. Instead of getting more specific about it, and looking closer, I lunged onward, doing only what I thought I knew. Something about Bruce Woolever must have worn off on me because when it came time to open my mouth and to say the words out loud, I found I had the courage. I could have sounded like a total idiot, and I probably did half the time, but I was good at being an idiot. I was convincing, and anyway I saw that making fun of myself was the surest way of doing this piece justice.

When my brother, who was suspicious of my intentions, asked me why I was trying out to go to *his* school, I said: "I'm already dumb, Joe. I can only get better at it."

For the next two weeks, I repeated that long list of ailments until I remembered their order exactly and the melodies they made in my ear. Then I counted the lines on the page, and decided I could give each line a different number. With the poem in hand, I began walking through the lines until I memorized the coinciding movements. The poem was about aches and pains, and so I began associating each line with different parts of my body as well, imagining what these fictional ailments felt like. The more I kept my mind busy with gestures and antics like this, the sooner the words seemed to come.

The book open, I rehearsed when to sneeze, how to cough, and at what pitch to whine. Each moment was prepared to seem both make-believe and believable. I waited before I coughed, and I took a second to judge myself whether or not it seemed *believable*. I ran through the house reciting. Once I could say each line of the poem without looking down, I went to sleep, telling myself that I was letting the poem sleep. Waking up again the next day, I did not pull back my sheets. Instead, I gripped them and looked up at the ceiling.

♦ ♦ ♦

It was raining on the day of my audition. My mother drove me to Norland Middle School, asking whether or not I had chosen the right shirt. It was a concert T-shirt for the Kinks. "It's the right shirt," I told her.

She shook her head. "I don't think you're right on this one."

"It's the piece I'm doing."

"What about it?"

"It's a comedy, Mom."

Coming into the auditorium, I saw my friend Bruce. He was center stage, and mid-performance. He leapt about, reciting lines to the left and to the right. Like me, he was doing a *girl's* monologue, but his was about Tinker Bell dying. The monologue itself had a reputation of being overdone but, as with "Sick," guys would never attempt it. Bruce skidded through the piece like he was peeling out in a drag race. He was showing off his long hair. I lowered my head and tried to keep from laughing out loud.

When he was done, I was almost crying. Bruce stood waiting for further instructions. "I'm finished!" He broke character. "So, how did I do? Like, did you like it? Pretty good, right? I practiced really hard on it. I had my sisters' help even." Mr. Wright, the drama teacher, asked Bruce to sit, waving him down. I thought Bruce would do as he was asked, lowering his head and taking the stairs, but he took the gesture literally and proceeded to walk off the edge of the stage. Mr. Wright leapt to his feet to stop him. It was a joke, of course! Bruce did not fall.

When my turn came, I requested two chairs. There were heavy stipulations against the use of chairs. I could use two only if my piece required both, and mine did. Before I stepped up onto the stage, I explained that I needed them to create the illusion of a bed. I showed Mr. Wright my sheets and pillow stuffed into a paper bag, and he waved to the stagehand: "Two chairs."

It was the only story I knew. I walked into the stage lights and found that I couldn't see until I turned my back to the house. I found my shadow scattered now in several directions around me. I sat down, stared into the lights, and put my feet up on the plastic seat of the other chair. I spread a sheet over my toes, and began: "'Sick,' by Shel Silverstein." The performance went exactly as planned. The words came easily, one line followed the next, and I convinced everyone present how much I hated school.

CHAPTER NINE

A Comedy

For my birthday the summer after sixth grade, my father presented me with an oversized present. He apologized that he couldn't wrap it and told me to close my eyes instead. This was sort of a big surprise. "No peeking."

"I won't peek, Dad."

He wasn't convinced. He needed a blindfold, so he grabbed a T-shirt that had been used some weeks ago to wash the boat. It had the logo of the college where he'd earned his master's degree in marketing, the University of Alabama. With this soap-stained jersey, he tried to wrap my face up so that he knew I couldn't see. I went with it. What else could I do? But the shirt wouldn't suffice, and so Dad went to the bathroom for a towel. When he got tired of messing with blindfolds, he put me in a headlock under his right arm and led me out the back door. He walked me around the table and chairs on the porch, and then said, "Okay, Travie; open your eyes. *Happy Birthday!*"

There hung a one-hundred-pound white canvas heavyweight punching bag. I was a 112-pound kid. The bag was suspended from a chain but not from the last link. My father set the height of the bag, hooking the chain six or seven links in. He did not cut off the remainder. I nudged the canvas, reading the logo as it spun: EVERLAST. "Is this for me?" I had never asked for a punching bag.

"Here are the gloves!" Each carried the same logo on the wrist. Dad waited until I put the matching gloves on and took a swipe at the bag. He even took a picture. "What do you think?"

He was handing me an edifice of my ignorance. In the moment, I was amused by his presentation, the whole headlock and dirty T-shirt masquerade, but this was my illiteracy he was wielding before me, and he was putting a happy face on it. The gloves were like platypus feet. On my hands, I felt like they were made of sand. I shook them off and left them on Dad's rusted weight-lifting bench. That afternoon, I asked my mother why I had been given a punching bag. She said it had been given to me as a kind of, she hesitated, therapy. She thought I'd like it.

"Why would I like it?"

She said I was coming into a period of confusion and, she thought, I might need some way to vent my unresolved feelings, my *adolescence*.

"I've been accepted into art school, Mom."

"Oh, I know."

"Why not give me something for art school?"

"Well," she said, dropping her voice, "it was your dad's idea."

I kept my mouth shut and decided to reject the punching bag altogether. I was no fool. Every day my parents would see that bag hanging, unmoved—a sign of their ignorance.

♦ ♦ ♦

That fall, for the first year in many, Joe and I left for school together. He was in the ninth grade and he was observably put off by the prospect of my tagging along behind him. The bus came early, making the turn from North Miami Avenue just as dawn was breaking. Joe stood before I did, asking, "You coming?" I grabbed my backpack, and we took our seats together. Looking out the window, I watched a light brown haze appear over the front lawns of houses I'd once pedaled past on bicycle. I could see differently, hear differently. I wondered whether or not my voices would travel with me to this new school or if some of them would be staying behind. I hadn't even made it to my first drama class, and yet something was changing in me. As a student of Norland, I now had permission to be creative and, in the name of art, to have my feelings.

As the bus climbed the on-ramp of the highway, other students and I looked out over the shining automobiles and sculpted concrete. The sunbeams were blinding. I turned around in my seat and found that my old friend Bruce Woolever was there, sitting quietly.

Norland was a big school, and it had all the troubles of any other school in Dade County. We were the students who made Norland different from other schools. As students in their "Cornucopia of the Arts," we took our academic classes with all the other kids in the morning, and in the afternoon we separated for drama, dance, art, or music.

Mr. Wright gave us a quick introduction on the first day of class. He promised us that through hard work and study each of us could one day be working actors. Then he went on to explain his first acting lesson. He gave us a demonstration of a pantomime technique called Neutral. It meant being present without emotion or, in more elementary terms, doing nothing. Mr. Wright said that Neutral was a difficult mental exercise. It required focus and discipline, which we would need if we wanted to make it in the theater.

I sat up in my chair, set my arms on the desk, and stepped out of myself. Neutral was no challenge for me. Once out here, beyond my frame, I felt like I was floating. I had no concentration to break. I could see all the people in class without moving my eyes. I could feel other students' thoughts pass through me. Mr. Wright looked down the aisles for a hint of a gesture, or a look in the eye, and he found none in me. I had simply set my voices, those I held in reserve, loose into the room about me. The next week we learned the Click, another pantomime technique that helped establish the illusion of objects. At our desks, in Neutral, we spent hours reaching into the air to create the illusion of holding a cup, a telephone, a fork, a balloon. This was called acting? Was acting the make-believe holding of a balloon? It all seemed like the most impractical education to me, and yet it was exactly how I had been experiencing the classroom until now: all artifice, choreography, show. Mr. Wright then began to arrange improvisations between students. He set up two chairs on the stage and explained that we should act out characters, miming all the properties in the scene. Our class played in make-believe shopping carts, carried make-believe briefcases, and held make-believe purse snatchings.

During the third week of classes, we were told that every student would be required to learn how to juggle. Mr. Wright said juggling made good stage business and would be an important skill to list on our résumés. To me, the spirit of juggling was like making fun of every other classroom. Nothing really mattered if you had the time to throw a few balls in the air.

When Mr. Wright brought in a professional clown, I knew I had made the right decision coming to Norland. The clown sprang up onstage and introduced himself, juggling three balls. He invited us to grab a set of socks from a box, and to repeat after him: "One, two, three. One, two, three." Socks flew everywhere, and the room fell apart with laughter. The juggler passed one of the colorful orbs beneath his leg and spun around, catching the others in one hand. Then he taught us the basic pattern, one ball at a time. While other kids threw their rolled socks at each other, I paid close attention. The clown paid close attention. After about ten minutes I discovered I could juggle two socks in one hand. By the end of class that day, I could juggle three in two hands and perform a number of tricks.

I came home and showed off in the living room. Dad was so excited that he asked me to show him how it was done. With a yawn, he said he'd always wanted to learn to juggle.

"Okay." I threw him a tennis ball and he caught it. I threw him another and he caught it with the other hand. Then I dared him to catch the third ball. He looked at me cautiously. "You've got to stand up," I told him. He did. "Don't anticipate. Wait for it," I said. Bravely, I explained every move. "Keep your shoulders relaxed. Try not to look at your hands." Dad raised an eyebrow like I'd need to watch my tone. In the next three afternoons, my dad learned how to keep three balls in the air, juggling. We stood across from each other in the living room passing them back and forth.

The next week, Mr. Wright revealed his grand design: the best four jugglers in class were going to be recruited into the school's "juggling troupe." He would spell the word *troupe* to make it sound like we were Italian minstrels, part of the commedia dell'arte.

To find out who were the best jugglers, we stood by our desks. Mr. Wright handed out socks and tennis balls from the box onstage. Once everyone had three, the test began. "One, two, three!" Socks flew up. Balls bounced. Some kids ran about their chairs screaming. Some ran into each other's way. If a student had dropped a ball he or she was expected to sit down. I stayed in my own kind of Neutral, juggling steadily. At some point, I felt like I was only waiting for the other kids to sit down. The moment I thought it, they did. Avi, Bruce, and Valerie sat down. When there were only four jugglers left, Mr. Wright introduced the new members of the juggling troupe: "Craig Reed, Adam Littman, Suzanne Young, and Travis Culley."

Together, we appeared to be four bright, lucky kids. Each of us took up our own role in the troupe: Craig, with the glasses, was the geek. Adam was the magician. I was the page. Suzanne was the princess. In many ways, the juggling troupe was a salvation for us. We bonded instantly, and would learn to develop our trust in each other. This saved us from the worry of cliques. I might have been the luckiest of the three because Craig, Adam, and Suzanne were some of the smartest young people I ever came to know. I admired them. I esteemed them, so I followed them outside with pins and rings and high hopes, and I tried to learn everything I could.

As jugglers, we were given a separate rehearsal schedule that extended to the end of the year. Instead of working on scenes, or doing improvisations, we spent our time in the yard behind the drama room, coming up with stunts that anyone would find amusing at the circus.

At home, I continued practicing. Mom even made me a special set of leopard-skin beanbags from a pillow that she'd cut up and stuffed with popcorn kernels. I told my father that juggling was all about restraint and repetition, timing and concentration. No matter how hard the trick, it must appear *relaxed*. This was something Craig taught me. "You can't be in a hurry or you'll mess up the timing." Dad got tired of it and had me go get him a beer. He was done.

In rehearsal, Mr. Wright developed a schematic arrangement of what we would do onstage. He would introduce us one by one, and we'd start our signature tricks. Then we'd go into more common tricks like juggling in one hand, passing under the leg, around the world. Mr. Wright carried a staff that was wrapped in ribbon and he narrated with a simple bullhorn. Finally, we would return to our individual talents and unveil our best stunts.

On performance days, we were excused from our classes and placed on buses with the equally exceptional girls from the dance department. On each of these field trips, the jugglers and dancers had something of a little party. There was no budget for costumes. The dancers wore black tights and assorted articles the department owned. Mr. Wright told us: "Wear something bright, you know? Something positive."

I asked Melanie next door what I should wear. She stood me in front of the mirror in her bedroom and had me mismatch my shoes and socks. I tried on some of her more colorful clothes. I showed up the next day wearing green pants, red suspenders, two contrasting plaid shirts, and Converse, mismatched blue and orange. Mr. Wright said I was the very essence of a clown.

As a group, we performed all over Miami. Some weeks we'd perform every other day, leaving school and returning before the last bell of the afternoon. I wasn't keeping up academically, but my performance schedule was the perfect excuse: I had juggling to do. With this, I received special treatment. I became a wiseass in the morning and a juggler in the afternoon. I seemed to brighten when my name was called. If I didn't have an answer, I would now say from the back of the room the first thing that came to mind, even if it was ridiculous.

On our way to performances, I sat next to Suzanne. She thought I was silly to stay in costume all day.

I defended my decision: "What's the difference? We perform all the time. Anyway, the world can be a shallow place."

CHAPTER TEN

Missing Persons

Every year my family was due to make a number of visits to see the grandparents in Daytona, "to shake the apples from the tree," Dad said. But this was Christmas Eve 1985, and Joe and I were being cautioned. Upon our arrival, Mom said, we would be meeting our uncle B.J., *her* brother, Bernard Joseph Fox.

"You have a brother?"

She laughed. "Well yes, Trav."

"Since when?"

"'Since when?' You actually met B.J. when you were a toddler, but you were probably too young to remember it."

"I'm twelve, Mom."

"That's why I'm telling you now, so you can prepare yourself, because today you are going to meet your uncle, and his family."

"Who are they?"

"Well, they live in Seattle. They have a five-year-old boy named Ryan. What do you want to know?"

"Who is Ryan?"

"He is . . . your cousin," she deduced. That was all. About his wife, her name was Joelle. Mom tried to describe her brother. He was tall, good-looking, charismatic, she said. I could sense her wondering how little she could say. She had virtually raised him from the time she was four years old, she said, and it shocked me. She'd fed him, changed him, and escorted him to school every day for "a quadrillion years." She'd begun working with him in Grandfather's bike shop when she was ten.

"Why haven't you ever told me about your brother before?"

"I don't know, Trav. *You never asked*."

"What are we going to give him?" my brother asked. "It's Christmas."

"Don't worry, I have ornaments for everyone already wrapped. We're going to be decorating Grandma's tree."

When we finally met our uncle, Joe and I stared up in amazement. He wore a white shirt, partly covered in coffee. The girl at the restaurant had spilled the pot onto his shoulder. B.J. had smiled and decided to wear the coffee stain home because he didn't have another clean shirt. And yet, he seemed to have everything. I met his wife and son. There was a sense of exhaustion and completion in him. He had nothing left but the joy he felt meeting us, and introducing Ryan to all the little objects in his mother's kitchen.

I looked at my mother, puzzled. Why had she kept him secret? She sighed and said nothing. After dinner, Ryan sat on B.J.'s knee, a little shy. Mom asked about the boy, and his ability to read. Joelle told us, "Ryan reads very well. He reads to us all the time." When the time came to open our ornaments and to decorate the tree, I opened two boxes with my name on them. In one box there was a juggler in a blue-and-white costume and a blue-and-white hat. In the other box was a set of masks, adjoining—the symbol of the theater—Comedy and Tragedy. Under the tree were matching black jackets from my dad, which Joe and I put on and wore about like mobsters.

On the drive home, the juggler in my lap, Mom said that B.J. had another family before this one, a wife, divorced now, and a child who had been put up for adoption. Who was this boy, where was he now? Mother kept silent. But then she never told us about the weddings, either one, or the births of our two cousins. The way my mother seemed to obliterate her brother, reducing him to single traits, made me nervous. My voices kept silent; they kept listening. Mother wasn't telling the whole story.

I had to acknowledge what I knew. My mother had thought she could keep her brother secret until our meeting became inevitable. It seemed she thought Joe and I would go on like nothing had ever happened, as if we were not quick enough to notice how removed we were from the other members of our family. I could see how carefully she'd withheld her brother's name. Prior to this, every day that she let a curse word slip, every day that she snickered at my choice of clothes, she'd never said a single word about my uncle—*or had she?*

We returned home late at night to find Gil mowing the front yard. Dad and Joe made jokes about how stoned he must be, and then my mother said those words again, but only barely, under her breath: "Reminds me of someone . . ."

I hung the masks up on my wall.

After winter break, classes were in session, and I went back to school with lots of energy. I don't know where it came from, but I didn't want to go home. I wanted to pretend that I didn't live at home. In Mr. Wright's class, I could. There was no difference between real and make-believe in an acting class, and no telling where I could go in a simple two-minute improvisation.

I began channeling voices, turning them into characters onstage. Ideas flooded my mind, and soon I had Adam and Valerie laughing. Acting was about being unreal, unlike life, and I found myself getting seated at the center of the action.

I came home with a smile on my face, a blush at times. I had a witty comeback for why I had not done my household chores. I had been trained to improvise, to leap into discussions unprepared, mocking my teachers and my audience, every one.

♦ ♦ ♦

One weekend, I found myself at home with my dad. It happened to be Easter. I'd been given a basket of candies. Now Dad called me out of my room. He didn't like getting up. His hair was out of control. He had sideburns and curls and a smudge of facial hair that had not quite grown into a mustache. "Have you finished packing yet?" he asked.

"Packing for what?"

"You're going to Daytona to see your grandparents."

"Again?"

"Tomorrow."

"Then shut up, Dad. *There's plenty of time.*" I said this like *C'mon. It's no big deal!* But he responded in one move. My father stood from his chair, grabbed my left arm, twisted it behind my back, and pushed me to the living room carpet. He said that I had been "trying him lately." He slapped me and punched me in the back, keeping a grip on my wrist like I was under arrest.

"Dad!" I shouted, and he dropped me. I tumbled through his feet, rolled to my heels, and ran to my room.

For a few minutes I waited behind my bedroom door. Then I heard his heavy footsteps approaching. I was prepared to run, either at him or around. He didn't knock. When he got to my door, he threw it open and started flicking the lights on and off. "I want you to understand something," he said. *"If you keep this up, son, you won't be my son anymore."* Then he left. I heard nothing but traffic.

He'd done this before, never to my brother, but to me. He thought he could get away with it, I guess. Maybe he thought he could do this to me anytime. What would I do about it? If I challenged him, or threatened him, he could hurt me more seriously and no one would know what had really happened here on this day.

I went over to my desk and found paper. With a pen I began to write down exactly what happened. I hurried, recording his exact words as best I could. Then I heard my father in the hall again, his footsteps quickly coming. I crumpled the paper and stuffed it under my knee. I held the pen tight when he came into the room. He stood there a moment and sighed. There was a commercial break. Dad sat down on the bed next to me and tried to say he was sorry, but he couldn't get all the words out right. I sat at the edge of my bed waiting for him to go, my face throbbing, my fists tense.

CHAPTER ELEVEN

The Absurd Hero

It is no secret that there is a relationship between children's performance in school and the hardships they are being expected to live at home. Given the terror of feeling that I might soon lose my father and mother, my name even, I had no more aptitude for literacy. I was too confused about who I was. My father never mentioned a divorce, so I thought I might be sent away, cast off—preemptively. This question rendered every sentence I would think beyond this one fragmentary. I was uncertain now of the worth of knowing something. In whose name would I know it? All that I did know and could point to was in a letter that I kept, and shared with nobody.

In whichever classsroom I sat, I watched the clocks. They disturbed me. The whole building had its clocks wired together so that it was always the exact same time in every classroom. I discovered this while walking the halls on my own, peeking into other classes. It made me curious, even suspicious. Time was not so orderly. Time went forward and back. Hours could be lost in a second, never to be recovered again. Hours could disappear entirely. What a silly illusion to think that the whole world might be set on the same dial like a flower that never blossomed. What a pointless exercise. As the day passed, I went from class to class with the bells, walking apace with these clicking wheels.

With the semester over, Dad wanted to send me and my brother back to church camp. He never said anything about God, mind you, but was insistent that it would be a good thing if Joe and I went. He said he wanted us to have *his* happy memories.

But then, on the last day of classes, Mr. Wright pulled me aside to tell me that he had decided to direct *Oklahoma!* for Norland's big summer musical. He added, in a whisper, that there might be a lead part in it for me.

"I don't have to go to summer school this year, do I?"

"No. This would only be if you want to, it would be completely voluntary."

I loved the sound of that: "completely voluntary." I checked in with my voices, and there was general agreement. I should definitely go to summer school. That night, I told my mother that I wanted to try out for the school play.

"In the summertime?" Mom asked.

"Why not?"

"What are they doing?"

When I announced the title, Dad turned and said, "*Yeah,* I don't know about this one, Paula."

When practice began, Mr. Wright handed me the script and I pulled him aside.

"Yeah, Trav. What's going on?"

"I just wanted to say that I'm nervous."

"What are you nervous about?"

I had to warn him. "I'm not very good at reading."

"Reading?"

I nodded. "I don't know how long it would take to memorize all this."

After a year of performances, and juggling lessons, Mr. Wright could never say he'd seen me reading. He blinked and said, "Okay. We'll work around it." Casting the roles that day, Mr. Wright made me a member of the chorus—the only member of the chorus. He had created a special part for me. No lines. I could be in almost every scene, and I would never have to sing as a principal, or memorize a word from the play. Others were happy to get the better parts. In the end, Avi Adler got the part of the lead cowboy, and I did not have to go to church camp.

Through the month of June some twenty kids, including many friends, met in the library for rehearsal. We opened the windows, moved the tables away from the center of the room, and set down pink tape to match the dimensions of the stage. Mr. Wright waved his arms at us, and made changes in the middle of the action. He pranced through the acting area, commanding our movements like a bandleader, pulling kids this way and that, three steps forward, or one step to the side. Mr. Wright expected us to sing, although none of us had ever had singing lessons. Like me, most of the kids had no idea of whether or not they were even on key. Another big point of confusion was whether Oklahoma, the state of Oklahoma, would require a *country* accent or a *southern* accent. This had to be discussed at length, because we were south of Oklahoma and we didn't have *southern* accents. Mr. Wright tried to answer, but suddenly Valerie, playing the flower girl, could not stop laughing.

As for me, I would come on and off the set with different props from a box, doing a series of puppetlike dances with ducks or horse heads on sticks of wood, or I was standing around with a straw cowboy hat over my nose, tapping my foot to the cassette tape orchestra. I was silent Jim, and this was all the choreography I needed to learn. I stood where I was told to stand, and tapped my foot.

That summer, after some discussion, my brother decided not to continue on with art school. He thought it a little girly to be an artist, and probably a little dumb. I mean, who makes much money drawing pictures? He was becoming someone who wanted the values of this world directly manifest. There was no place for imitation. He wore a real leather jacket and a real gold chain that he'd lifted from the store where he worked at the mall. He hid his weight behind oversized T-shirts and meticulously combed his hair like he was shaking off an insult.

♦ ♦ ♦

On the first day of eighth grade, I stepped onto the bus alone. I greeted the driver, Mrs. Ingram, and walked straight to the back. There, I sat down across from Bruce and started catching up. We talked about the summer that had passed and laughed our way to school. Also on our new route were a few new kids in the art department: Chris and James. Chris wore inked Vans, a black denim jacket, and checkerboard tights that he stole from his sister. James yelled profanities out the window and tagged the seats with a permanent marker. Bruce wore his hair long, torn jeans. I wore three pairs of sunglasses, another broken pair of mismatched Chuck Taylors, and a hat with three brims that had been sewn together with shoelaces. Why not? This was art school. The point was to stand out. Art school seemed the only place for us; either that or the loony bin, Mrs. Ingram would say. At the front of the bus sat Valerie, a bow in her hair.

After academic classes, I went to the acting room, expecting to see Mr. Wright. When I opened the door, ready to make my big entrance, I met our new drama coach, Mrs. Chavers. She sat us down in front of a television and said she was going to show us what "serious theater" was. Things were going to be different, she said, "measurably." There would still be a juggling troupe, but it would not be performing every week like before.

I stopped listening. I felt this irk in my stomach. When her introduction was over and the attendance had been taken, Mrs. Chavers pressed a button on the console of the television, and up came a scene from the Samuel Goldwyn production of *Oklahoma!* Half the class chuckled. Was this our "serious theater"?

No one sang the lyrics or spoke their lines. No one claimed their parts. No one admitted that it was the same musical we'd done that summer, not even Avi. Before she turned it off, I inspected the scenes for quiet cowboy Jim. He wasn't there.

Because of the way I dressed, I think Mrs. Chavers took me for a troublemaker. No one else came to class prepared to break every rule and norm. But then, she had a lot to prove. Wasn't she already upsetting traditions that we had set in place? Who was the troublemaker? We couldn't tell each other apart.

The next day, we weren't taught mime techniques. Instead, Mrs. Chavers told us that we didn't know the first thing about being theater artists. She went around the room, asking, "What is theater?"

Valerie started: "Theater is imitation."

Adam added: "Theater is performance."

Bruce chimed in: "Theater is play."

Mrs. Chavers interrupted. "Theater is conflict." Then she asked us if we knew what the elements of theater were.

"Elements?"

"What does every play have in common?"

"Actors?"

"Scenes?"

"Dialogue?"

"Action," she answered. "Every play has a beginning, a middle, and an end. And what happens in the middle?"

"A climax," I said.

"Right, a climax of the *conflict*. And what happens with the *conflict*?"

"The conflict becomes resolved," Avi offered.

"Right. Something happens. So, what are your favorite plays?"

The class went silent.

"Come on, you've got to have favorites. What are they?"

The class sat still, and said nothing.

"How many plays have you read?"

No one responded. Mr. Wright had never asked us to read a play before. A few scattered titles were mentioned. She shook her head. "You've *got* to read plays if you are going to be actors in the theater. Who has worked on scenes from a play?"

"We were doing improvisations," Elaini said.

"Improvisations? All year?"

She smiled.

"What did you do last year?"

My best answer was juggling, so I kept quiet.

"Have you done any Method training?"

Silence.

"Alexander Technique? Linklater? Strasberg? You've never heard of these people, have you?"

"We know Marcel Marceau," Michelle answered with a dose of irony.

"Well, in this class we are going to be reading plays, and talking about plays, and working on scenes and monologues from plays." Mrs. Chavers handed us a big plastic bucket that was full of little books, each with the same cover, and the name Samuel French. Our first assignment was to pick one play from the bin and to read it. Then we would find a two-person scene, and match up with another student in class.

I pulled out of the box at random *A Radio Play*. It took place in a recording studio in the 1920s. Scene One opened with a guy doing commercials that were full of screeches and sound effects. Other students were sitting quietly in their seats holding their plays up, and I suddenly had a realization: *reading* in Mrs. Chavers's class was no different than going into Neutral in Mr. Wright's class. She wasn't asking us to read but to act like we were reading plays. She wanted us to sit here and do nothing! I turned the page, and went into Neutral.

Mrs. Chavers was right. I did face a real conflict. If I wanted to be an actor, I would need to read plays.

Some kids had years of practice. I supposed that everyone knew how to separate their ideas from those they received from reading, but I didn't. And now there were many characters I was having to entertain. How was I supposed to tell them apart? Or keep them together? My characters had no barriers. They came and went as they liked. They spoke for themselves. *Maybe I was meant to be something different than an actor*, I thought as Mrs. Chavers paced on the boards. Maybe I should be a stand-up comedian, maybe a host or entertainer. Perhaps I was better on my feet, improvising, rather than plowing through all the parts of a tragedy. My life would be easy. Parts would find me. I had my own virtues and special qualities. I could feel what I wanted to feel, I could make my imagination come alive at any moment. I could believe anything I imagined. Everything was permitted. These voices came and went out of the background, and onward, like a dream, they would go on disregarding Mrs. Chavers, disregarding everything.

I looked back down at the script in front of me: *A Radio Play.* Maybe I could be a radio announcer! I inspected the cast list. Then came a scene description. In some ways, I was still pretending, timing out my pantomime, but in other ways, I began scanning the action of the scene. I let my eyes fall on the words. They seemed to hang from the fold. The words worried me, so I tried to see around them. I tried to see the exterior, following the directives, names. On the page, I perched around the edges, playing with the margins in my mind—"scene," "Voice One," "lights up," "On Air"—admitting to what I could not deny.

There were three characters, each named by number. They were recording a toothpaste commercial, two girls and a guy making some commotion: *"Shuga shuga!" "Pop!" "Mmwaaww!"* The play descended into onomatopoeia, and I kept daydreaming about unusual percussion instruments. I was amused, but over nothing. It was as if my voices had developed their own radio show for a moment, but then they'd divert the drama, going way off track.

Mrs. Chavers told us to take our plays home and finish them for homework. Leaving class, I quietly tossed *A Radio Play* back into the box where it came from.

That year my grades fell way below average. I didn't care. I was talking in Mr. Wade's Social Sciences class. When the teacher interrupted me, I became offended. He was incensed by my reaction. I spent an hour in detention for that. In English, I came to class unprepared. I took incompletes on my assignments. Some teachers took pity on me. Others didn't.

When I brought my report card home after winter break, I didn't even look at it. Mom showed me three Ds, one in

Drama, one in Phys Ed, and another in Algebra. Mrs. Chavers didn't like me, and I didn't like my Algebra teacher. Mom warned me that I would have to get serious about my grades if I hoped to remain a *gifted* student.

"And what if I don't want to go to school at all?"

"Do you think you can make it on your talent alone?"

"I don't think I have a choice, Mom."

"Well, then I give up. I can't help you," she said, walking away. "You can go on and be illiterate for the rest of your life, and you'll suffer the consequences."

♦ ♦ ♦

In Algebra, I saw numerals scrambled on the chalkboard behind Mr. Orsini. I balked. He was a small, older man with thick, dark hair, who looked like an accountant. He wore short-sleeved button-down shirts and a gold watch. He rarely left his seat. He read from the book. He opened no discussions about the application of algebra in the world outside of math. He gave no explanations of how letters were being used in equations, no deliberations on the higher meaning of the powers of division. I remember when he first used the word *variable*. A variable was a letter, and a letter could be a number. "What is the variable *a* in this equation?"

Was he talking about the *a* in *algebra*? He could not control how I could misunderstand him. I was the variable. On my next test, I made a classic tree pattern, slaying sheep all the way down the page. I turned my random answers in with the others and left class with resolution. I had solved the equation.

Throughout the year, Mr. Orsini had given me two Ds,

and an F in conduct that could not be changed unless I took the whole course over again. Mrs. Chavers also gave me a set of Ds that were costly. By mail, I was given notice that I was no longer welcome at Norland Middle School and that I would be sent to my regional school, Thomas Jefferson Junior High, for the ninth grade.

Bruce moved on ahead without a goodbye.

CHAPTER TWELVE

Gang Theory

My rejection from Norland hit home. I didn't get much sympathy, but then my family thought I was only getting by on luck, and as long as I did, I seemed more curious to them. Someday all my luck would have to come crashing down. After all, I still hated reading, and that meant I was the same illiterate loser they'd always thought I'd be.

I didn't ask for help. Instead, I stopped watching TV. I spent my evenings on the back porch taking punches at the canvas bag that my dad had given me. *Therapy*. Each punch cut into my apple-white fists, sending home flashes of pain that went right up my elbows and into my shoulders—making my jaw clench. The bag was too big for me. I walked in a slow circle around it, shaking out my hands. I bent my knees and eyed the canvas. I coached myself—*punch through the bag*—and sent a fist flying. On contact, a shot of pain; I stood back and tried again. While the rest of the family sat inside and watched television, I would get the bag rocking, swinging, bouncing—if I could hit it with the right combination. That small length of chain rang through the house. My father heard the sound all weekend, all night, and even in his sleep. I kept slugging at the canvas until, exhausted, rocking side to side on the heels of my high-tops, I would reluctantly step away.

♦ ♦ ♦

On the first day of school in September, stepping inside the main hall of Thomas Jefferson Junior High, I felt like I was invisible. Even with my painted shoes and red knuckles, other kids crowded the halls and walked into me. The students were much worse than I had expected. T.J. was nothing like Gil had described it. The majority of the students seemed to think that the only way of getting by was by keeping up defenses and intimidating people.

At T.J. there were few gifted types, and only a handful of kids who identified as artists. In art class, there was no dance, or acting, or musical theater. We worked with paper and glue, just like in the fourth grade.

The school did have a marching band, but there were no blues ensembles or jazz quartets. At band practice, kids would get dressed up in gray and gold marching uniforms and twirl wooden guns. The rest of the year the school felt like a network of tunnels. The halls echoed between classes.

Rooms were so full that I sometimes doubted that I would be able to get out in an emergency. On every piece of furniture, in every door and wall, there were signs of emergencies past, an ongoing sense of barely restrained panic. Even my English teacher, Mrs. Seitlin, seemed to fear the doors of the classrooms. Throughout homeroom and first period she would look back at the doors to be sure they were closed.

I sat down in my assigned seat in a room of thirty teenagers, ashamed to know nobody. The desks were arranged in rows, and students were assigned to them alphabetically. In Mrs. Seitlin's class, if you were not in your seat by the time the bell rang, then you were marked absent. If you collected too many absences you would fail her class. If you did not accept the conditions, more conditions would be imposed on you. I kept to myself and reserved my judgments.

Every morning, Mrs. Seitlin would begin by taking roll.

"Marcia Arollo?"

"Here."

"Faisal Assad?"

"Here."

"Quintana Baker?"

"Here."

"Maria Cartega?"

"Here"

"Travis Culley?"

I raised a finger.

"Eugene Gregory?" Her pencil flicked back and forth as she made marks in a leaf-green book. She read announcements from a printed newsletter and went over the rules of the class. The disciplinary procedures came first, academic expectations came second. She had rules about what to do if you had a problem with an assignment, how to be called on in class, even when to go to the bathroom. It was not okay to speak unless you had raised your hand.

In the middle of the classroom, there was Merle, a kid with big hair and tufts of sideburns that someone his age wasn't supposed to have yet. On the other side of the room there was a kid named Desi, who desperately wanted to be the class clown. On my side of the room was Ray, who was innately much funnier. The whole year there would be some contention about who was the real class clown.

Behind me sat a tall quiet kid with brown hair hanging over his face. He wore a straw hat more suited to Jimmy Buffett than to Axl Rose, but he decorated it with buttons from his favorite bands: Nirvana, Guns N' Roses, Judas Priest, and Ozzy Osbourne. His name was Eugene John Gregory *the Third*, but he went by Gene-John.

After homeroom, we moved right on to discussions of literature. Who was the subject of literature? I zoned out. By the end of the hour, Mrs. Seitlin had issued our first homework assignment. She told us to bring in "a paragraph on the subject of"—she paused, holding us in some suspense—"what you each did last summer." When these predictable words came out of her mouth, a certain intangible disappointment fell over the whole classroom. We felt betrayed. I shook my head, understanding that this class might as well already be over with. I was not going to learn anything here, and neither would anyone else.

Gene-John raised his hand.

"Yes? Eugene."

"What is a paragraph?"

She answered the question without breaking focus. "At least five sentences," she said. I was tempted to ask her what a sentence was, but I thought it too ridiculous. My literacy was the very last thing I wanted, in any show-and-tell sense, to share with a classroom of strangers. Then the bell rang, signaling the end of first period. We had to collect our stuff.

In my room, I tried to come up with five basic statements about what I had done this summer. What did she care? It all seemed so ridiculous. I had been kicked out of Norland this summer. I couldn't write about that. My next-door neighbor Melanie had moved away. It broke my heart. I couldn't write about that. I thought about other details from the summer: I had gone back to church camp while my brother went to Washington, D.C. It was a painful experience full of awful thoughts. I could never write about that.

I wrote about summer school. Algebra, Typing, and the punching bag: I had a brutal summer. Everything that the assignment brought up in me broke my pride, and for different reasons. For some time, I could not even touch a sheet of paper with my pen without breaking it in frustration. To complete the assignment, I wrote down what words I could easily spell, scribbling one sentence about going boating in the Florida Keys, and one about coming home. I wrote three sentences about beating the Everlast punching bag.

Mom said, looking down at my assignment, "How can you write a paragraph if you can't even write a sentence?" I snapped the page out of her hands and went back to my room. I affirmed my detachment from these things. I would learn when it became necessary, not a moment sooner.

I turned in my assignment folded in fours and Mrs. Seitlin stopped me. She unfolded my paragraph. "Excuse me," she said. "How am I supposed to read this?" I could hardly read it myself. My paragraph was a crumpled mass of scratches and parts of words that had been scribbled out and replaced by others.

"This is unacceptable," she said.

"Why?" I asked.

"It's so messy! Look at how the other kids' papers are! Do you see a difference?"

"But *I* wrote it!"

She glared. "Okay. I'll let it go this time, but next time, try to make it cleaner." I returned to my seat, opened my folder, and brushed the incident off.

As we sat through class, I began to get distracted by the writing being done by Gene-John. While I stared at the walls, and listened to dramas unfold in my mind, he spent the whole hour writing in a blue binder that was stuffed with lined paper. He wore his hat in class, lowered his head over the desk, and scribbled out continual lines of ink without going back.

"What are you doing?" I asked in a whisper.

He kept writing. At the end of the hour, he wrote me back on a little piece of paper: *Writing.*

What are you writing?

Letters.

That day, after the bell, we talked about it:

"What kinds of letters are they?"

"I don't know if I can answer that."

"Well, who are the letters for?"

"I am not sure they're meant to be read by anyone."

This made me curious—not to read what he had written, but to see what writing was for him, what kind of a secret art it had become. I asked him to clarify: "If they are letters, someone ought to read them."

He said that he was writing letters, like letters to himself, to develop his letter-writing skills.

"Well, I don't get it."

He couldn't explain it.

After lunch we would meet up in the courtyard to kick around a footbag. Ray and Desi would join in. Gene-John and I faced off against each other, trying for the most kicks and the splashiest tricks. We all maintained some conversation while delicately, or clumsily, kicking the footbag from person to person. If it went all the way around, we celebrated. Everyone who played in took credit for the round. Desi taught us the rules: no hands, and no apologies.

One day Gene-John turned to me in the courtyard and said, "This is a prison, you see?"

"They call it a free country, Gene-John."

"Look around you. Who can leave? Can you? Where could you go?"

"Maybe I could jump that fence right there."

"And then where would you go?"

"Anywhere. What are you saying?"

"I mean, does anyone have a life here, or a future? We're all prisoners in this system."

"Even the security guards?"

"Especially the security guards."

Gene-John's dad had been a POW in Vietnam. He had a theory that the public school system was only designed to make workers and soldiers, functionaries, security guards.

"No one here is going to succeed for being original, don't believe it. School is all about being part of a group, and if you are not part of a group or a gang of some kind, the school won't even know what to do with you." Gene-John laughed. He had a cackle that was a little insane.

"What are you saying?"

"If they failed us, and kept us here, we wouldn't really learn anything new, would we? Another year would pass and they wouldn't have anything new to teach us, would they?"

"Probably not."

"So if we failed, another time, like a third or a fourth round, they'd start running out of places to put us. We would just get older. Think about it, we'd be weirder than anyone!"

"So, at some point, they're going to have to pass us? Is that what you're saying?"

"No matter what we do, or don't do. As long as we are part of a group, they will move us through the program as a group. Only the really, really unique ones, those who will not fit into any group, will get held back. And it doesn't matter if you can't write. It doesn't matter if you can or can't read a book! In fact, most people don't read books." He laughed. "If you want to be part of a big group, don't read anything at all."

"I don't," I acknowledged.

"Then congratulations, you're part of a group."

CHAPTER THIRTEEN

Path of Sons

In first period, while Mrs. Seitlin was talking about our reading assignment, a chapter from the *Odyssey,* I wrote Gene-John a note in green ink: *She doesn't know anything.*

He wrote back in blue: *And what else is new?*

"So who is Telemachus looking for in this chapter?" I looked around. No one dared to raise their hand. She started again. "Telemachus is on a journey; he's going to travel around the world searching. Can anyone tell me who Telemachus is looking for? Gene-John, how about you?"

He sat up: "His father?"

"Yes, his father. Very good, Gene-John."

I had to laugh. I was sure he was guessing. He'd probably

said the first thing that came to his mind. Mrs. Seitlin continued her lecture, looking back to our corner of the room whenever she needed affirmation. She had confidence that Gene-John had read the material. He returned to his writing, cracking a little smile. I was amazed. I was seeing that writing really served two functions: it protected him from our teacher's suspicions, and it secured, for her, Mrs. Seitlin, the illusion that Gene-John was actually paying attention. He wasn't paying attention. He was writing.

After lunch, walking back to class, Gene-John was right behind me when a fist came out of the crowd and hit him in the ear. A small tough kid named Vinny was brandishing knuckles. But then another kid stepped up and slugged my friend in the stomach. Ray and I stood back as Gene-John bent over and let five boys punch at his back and tear at his clothes. Gene-John covered his head with his arms. One part of the crowd cleared away, and another part piled on. There had been no notice, and no motive for the attack.

Then, from beneath the pile of his assailants, Gene-John stood up, throwing kids off of him in two directions. He went mad, swinging at anyone he could see. He threw a punch that knocked one kid right into the wall. Someone leapt on his back and wrapped his arms around him. Tall Gene-John began swinging about, kicking at the others, carrying one of these thugs on his back. With one hand free, he grabbed the guy riding him. Then he turned and body-slammed him onto the concrete floor. Gene-John was like a monster. He seemed invincible until two security guards tackled him and dragged him up to the principal's office.

After that day, Gene-John's personality changed sharply.

He lost all of his shy smiles and humorous asides. In homeroom he'd become cruel with Merle, even with Ray. We'd all sit together in the cafeteria. When Ray brought his tray to the table, Gene-John pulled the chair from beneath him—just to make us laugh. When Ray fell, Gene-John's cackle echoed off of the walls and tables. We were all a little afraid for our friend. He was no longer the gentle punk rocker he used to be. Whatever he had become, we had no handle on him now.

Then we started stealing lunches. At first, it was a small habit, like a gag. Gene-John would duck out of line with his lunch tray as I was approaching the lunch lady. I'd provide cover by paying the lunch lady in coins. It was easy. A week later, I began to discover ways of stuffing extra chocolate milks into my unzipped backpack. Every time through the line, the maneuver became simpler, until the table where we sat began to look like a feast of free food, extra sandwiches and shared desserts. We'd pig out, hold absurd conversations, and then we'd head out to the courtyard and kick a footbag.

Vinny appeared. He ran into the circle, grabbed the leather Hacky Sack we were kicking, and threw it onto the roof of the athletic department. No one moved. Then Vinny ran around the courtyard expecting to be chased.

Desi pulled out his knit bag, and the rest of us resumed playing.

Gene-John walked slowly over to Vinny: "That was mine."

"So?" Vinny said, coming closer.

Gene-John was ready to fight, but more inclined to play.

He looked down at Vinny and started laughing, pointing. Everyone looked. Ray and Desi laughed, and as others joined them, Vinny brightened. *"What is it? So what?"* He did not comprehend the attack.

Those days at T.J. stretched out like aeons as I tried to comprehend how to laugh at my own grief, laugh at the idea of the failure of coming here, laugh at the next obstacle set before me. That was the penultimate lesson that Gene-John taught me. There really was no other way. One rainy Monday, Gene-John and I decided to leave after homeroom and ditch for the rest of the day. We spent a few hours at the Cloverleaf Gameroom, then we took a bus to Haulover Beach. It was desolate, and cold. The rain was warmer than the wind. We found cover in view of the boardwalk and talked about some of the things we weren't learning in school.

"Have you ever been afraid of your father?" I asked Gene-John.

"No. Well, yes but no. I wish he wouldn't do things the way he does sometimes, so I think he should be feared. But I am not *afraid* of him. Why?"

"My dad is at home right now waiting to beat me up."

"You mean, now?"

"Yes, right now."

"What for?" Gene-John asked.

"I don't know. He does this. I only know he's waiting."

"Is he drunk?"

"He is, probably."

"Don't go."

"Don't go home?"

"What can he do?"

"He can call the police and say I'm missing. He probably would."

"So what? You can call the police too. That's self-defense."

"I don't want that."

"Can you defend yourself?" Gene-John asked.

"No."

"Well, good luck, man. Look into the wind," he said, pointing to the horizon.

"Face the music?" I answered, tapping my temple. We knew without saying, this was the path of sons.

♦ ♦ ♦

Coming home, I found my father stationed in his chair as usual. The television was on but he was barely seeing beyond the frames of his glasses. He asked me if I had cleaned my room.

"My room is clean, Dad." It was probably not the best answer.

"Go clean it again."

"Okay, Dad." I restrained myself. "I'll go clean my room again." I turned and walked away from my father nervously. My floor was clean. My desk was organized. I found an old cassette tape, Devo. Holding my breath, I broke the tape over my knee and pulled the reels out. There was a small fan in my room. Soon, I was tying tape to the fan cage. When I turned the fan on, pieces of tape went fluttering about, tickling my face. Looking into it, I heard my laughter echo back to me, cut into pieces.

I did not hear my father coming. Suddenly the door flew open and Montezuma was standing above me red-faced and arms crossed. I stopped the fan. The little pieces of tape lost their dancing energy and slowly drifted down to the carpet. "I told you to clean your room," he said, "not mess it up." I blocked a forceful slap that had been meant for my face, and then I got hit with the other hand. I grabbed his wrist. He threw me back to the ground and stepped closer. "You can't even get *that* right." He twisted my arm and hit me in the face, mouthing the words "Simple instructions." I tried to kick, and he turned me over, pushing my ear into the carpet. He gave three blows to the back of my head. I tried to block them but my effort was just a display. "I'll teach you to disobey your father," he said, wrenching my arm.

"Stop, Dad!"

He looked at me, squeezing.

"Stop, Dad! Stop!" It was my voice. He let go, flipped off the light, and slammed the door. I heard him walking through the house and sitting in his corduroy chair. I started replaying the events. I found that the carpet beneath me was a collection of clues, footprints and scuffs. Only I knew how to read them.

When Joe came home around seven, I took my shoes off and carefully walked down the hall in my socks. I made no sound. When I came to my brother's door, I knocked quietly.

Joe cracked the door. "Dad beat me up again," I said to him in a breath. My brother knew about other times. "He came into my room and started hitting me." I turned to show him the red marks on my neck, and Joe shut his door in my face.

I walked back to my bedroom thinking about how much harder it would be from this day forward, without a supportive father, or a brother. I gazed into the eyes of the zebra in my wallpaper. I wondered if I had a mother.

The sound of her car coming home woke me; beams of her headlights flashed across the faces of animals. I heard the car door shut and the trunk open. I got up, hurried down the hallway, and met her in the living room.

Dad was there. Mom saw my eyes. "Travie, what's wrong?"

I told her.

"That's not how it went," Dad said from his chair.

"*Yes it is!*" I replied, little hero.

"Travis, come here," he demanded. "Come here. *Now!*"

I stood behind my mother and held her arm. Dad stayed in his chair. Mom tapped my shoulder. "It's okay, honey. Go to your bedroom, dear."

From my bedroom window I could see my parents talking. Dad turned the television down. They spent the hour talking about their relationship. Dad said he was only here for the kids, to give us a "father figure." If he couldn't do that, he asked, "what's the point of playing along?"

The next day, I told Gene-John all about what happened. He said I should start taking Tae Kwon Do.

"Then he would really punish me."

"Well, what's the worst thing you can do to him?"

"Write about him. He hates embarrassment." Then I pointed at the blue binder under his arm. "I need one of those."

"Well sure, make one!"

In homeroom, while Gene-John wrote in his binder, I began writing in a sort of journal that I had bought from an art supply store. This would be my first writing experiment. The book was thin and simple, but it was bound, and it came with clean ruled pages. I wrote with a four-in-one ballpoint pen that allowed me to change color for every entry. With a little button I could go from blue to green, green to red, and red to black. I never wrote in cursive.

While Mrs. Seitlin lectured, I clung to my pen. I wrote about myself, recording the basic details first. I had no familiar words. I wasn't curious about those I could easily draw from. I was looking for the right words, not merely appropriate words. If I had to invent them or change them to fit my life, I would. If I had to write them again, in red and blue and green, I would. I wrote about my father beating me. I wrote about living in a house without love, never trusting anybody. I described how all the structures around me were fragile, and failing. I changed the color of my ink. I didn't know when it would take place, or how it would happen, but I knew that I would soon be writing about the dissolution of my family and the separation of my parents. If I did not begin writing, going one step beyond the letter I'd written on Easter, there would be no way of ever going back to that point and adding up all the details. There would be no way to know how I fell so far outside of a good family and a normal life. I penned these ideas in red and green and let them sit. *No bodies perfect.*

It may have been my most disobedient moment, writing about my family—even on page one. I should have been taking notes in English. Luckily, while writing, I found I wasn't being called on. Mrs. Seitlin stopped looking in my direction. In Science and in Home Economics, the same was true.

No matter what I was doing, my teachers thought I was following directions as I set my pen to the page in another color.

♦ ♦ ♦

Only two days after I began this journal, still on page one, I came home from school and found the back door of Dad's car open. I closed it. I found the kitchen door open, and I found the kitchen empty. I walked into the dining room and saw a shadow in the hall. Dad, in his moccasins, met me at the door of his bedroom and said: "Don't just stand there. Make yourself useful." I put down my backpack and started carrying his things to the car. He told me to get his shaving stuff together and to put it in a paper bag, but I wouldn't do it. I refused. I wasn't going to go into his bathroom, and I did not want to touch his shaving cream. "That's all right," he said. "Then go into the pantry and fill up a few bags of food."

"What kind of food?"

"Whatever: snacks, canned food, pasta—*whatever your dad likes to eat*." The whole time I couldn't help but sense that there was something planned about his behavior. He was still moving about in his head like he was going through a checklist, packing essentials into a pillowcase.

CHAPTER FOURTEEN

A Tragedy

There is always a way to do something wrong. It's often good to explore this. I might have told my parents what had happened at camp. I didn't. I might have learned to spell a certain word incorrectly and for many years not caught it. What is the difference between "staring" and "starring"? Likewise, I might learn to see something incorrectly. I might look back at my childhood home, later in my life, and not recognize it. All this is possible. People err in every aspect. Other people in our environment can effectively expand this principle. Think about it: if one person can misunderstand society, there must be hundreds of ways to misunderstand a person.

What I've learned is that literacy is a reflection of a need to document experience. We develop writing to keep record of changes that are happening around us. Writing is real. It is a form of calibration. We follow logic, likeness, and step forward, carefully, from one understanding to a new understanding. Restraint and imagination are both necessary to the process because it always requires some investigation to be sure of making a comparison.

In the process of reading, there is an exchange that takes place between our projected fears and the forms that take shape to perception. A reader has to be ready for anything. While language may be generative, literacy is reductive. That is why one must be prepared for a reading that haunts them.

Imagine that something terrible happens. A child is taken away, the mind looks on the scene with surprise, sees the absence as a disaster. The absence is terrifying. So our eyes become trained to notice small changes—to better watch over our children as they sleep. Our eyes become trained to recognize the faces of our own so that they can be called by their names when they rise. Reading involves recognition and fear. We rest our eyes a moment and look back, careful not to see too deeply or too shallowly.

Literacy always has an object. The difference between literacy and illiteracy is then a matter of how a person handles words, reading them or writing them down. The literate respect pages, and use them, gathering together the important propositions they make. The literate will tire a chapter out and wear it down to obviousness. When confused, the literate will acknowledge their confusion and trace their way back to where that confusion began.

♦ ♦ ♦

I never did figure out my father, and I feel like he left the house without having really met me. The story of my broken family, clumsily written, began on page two of my journal in black.

On the third and fourth pages I wrote about school, my brother, movies I'd seen. I needed to do some catching up. In colors, I began to write about other people that I had an aversion toward. I explored my feelings. Doing so helped me take my mind off of heavier subjects. Sometimes, I tried to describe what was happening in school or in my imagination. Sometimes, I wrote down words I heard around me: quotes from the sky, or the classroom, or the cafeteria. I changed the color of the ink and started a new line. I could sense that there was some kind of magic involved in documenting someone's exact choice of words—even my own. I recalled my father's words. He'd lived up to them exactly.

When I came home from school, I left my punching bag alone. For one morning, maybe two, there was nothing to keep hidden. Joe and I looked at each other eye to eye. Dad was not there anymore to reinstate the privilege of the first-born. And, given all my "therapy," my brother had become less willing to pester me. He'd seen me hit the punching bag so hard that it flew off its rings and crashed to the limestone. I had done this three times before. Now, I sat at the dining room table, looking at the house from new perspectives, feeling long streams of fresh air pass through the screens and blinds.

Joe was wearing designer jeans now, and driving a sports

car that Dad had bought him for his birthday. It was a vintage Camaro with rust under the fenders, and a small spoiler under the back window. It had racing grips, but no radio. Mom had put the house on the market. We would soon sell the property, the boat, and we'd sell my punching bag for a few dollars at a garage sale.

After a lean Thanksgiving, Mom came home from her part-time job and found a large white box on the kitchen table. It was a mystery. The box had been addressed to my brother, Joe, but there was no return address. By the red stamp in the corner Mom could see that it had been shipped from Washington. "Seattle, Washington," she said. "B.J. must have sent this. It must be some kind of gift." The white box sat on our table for a week. Then it moved to a chair. When the pine tree went up by the window, the white box was waiting.

Broken with curiosity, Joe opened the box a week before the holiday. Inside, without wrapping, Joe found a used Kenwood radio. It looked like it had been pulled out of someone else's dashboard. There was no card or note attached, no instructions. The mystery was only growing, and it seemed to make fools of all of us.

After Christmas Day came and went, the radio still waited. The cardboard box was folded in the kitchen with the trash.

Then, two days later, Mother received a call from B.J.'s wife to see if we had learned anything of her brother's whereabouts. He'd been missing for more than twenty-four hours. Mother tried to hide her worry. "B.J. may have a girlfriend," she offered. "Perhaps he doesn't want to be found." She said anything she could think to say, and the mystery only grew.

When my dad came to the house to visit, he took Joe to get the radio installed—but it didn't work. The technician gave the dead crab back to my brother, and Dad bought him a lesser radio. Now, everyone had questions for B.J., but no one between Miami and Seattle knew where he was. Mother said he'd fallen off of a cliff.

♦ ♦ ♦

By the morning of New Year's Day 1988, our worries seemed to have settled. The cat sat up on the counter where Dad would leave his keys and coins. Mom made a cup of coffee and began reading the Sunday *Miami Herald*. There, on the front page, was a story about a young arts conservatory designed for high school kids in public school. The story caught my mother's attention.

The school had opened the previous September and was now putting out a call for auditions to fill its second generation of students from tenth to twelfth grade. I was astonished by the pictures. Mother read the name from the headline: "New World School of the Arts."

"I want to do that," I said, looking over her shoulder.

"You've tried that, haven't you?"

"Different school, Mom."

She tried to level with me. "Don't you think your chances of getting in will be affected by the fact that you were kicked out of your previous gifted program?"

"Students will be accepted on their auditions," I said, paraphrasing.

"*If* they accept you."

"It's really not up to them," I reasoned. "It's up to me."

My mother looked down sharply. In a few weeks, we began filling out the application forms for New World School of the Arts. Like before, Mother told me what to write. I carefully penned the words into their spaces after having each one approved, making sure they were all spelled right. When each of the questions had been answered, my mother went through a list of requirements, circling the last word on her list: "Transcripts."

Mom relaxed. She could go by Norland after work and pick them up from the office. This sounded easy enough, but then I remembered her theory of self-sabotage, and I took it out of her hands. "School is over at two-thirty. I don't think there is going to be anyone in the office if you go by after work."

"I can leave early."

"Can you get there by two-thirty in the afternoon?"

"No, that's unreasonable."

"Then you can't get this done."

"It is an office. They've got to keep office hours, don't they?"

"No they don't."

"I'll call them."

"They won't listen to you." She started to say something. "I won't listen to you."

She blinked.

The next morning, I left the kitchen with a note from my mother permitting me to leave school midday. I thought I was prepared, but I hadn't eaten. I'd spent the morning hungry, nervous about my next move. Then, after the second hour, I walked out of the rear doors of the school building and crossed the catwalk over the highway. No one saw me. On the other side, I walked along an access road beside a row of small homes and emerged beside a bus stop on Seventh Avenue. It was a quiet day. The driver let me aboard. I got off the bus a few blocks from Norland Middle School and walked the rest of the way. Classes were in session. I stepped into the administration hall and talked to a woman in the office. She gave me a sealed envelope. There was no fee. I turned, and I began my journey home.

Getting off the bus on 152nd Street, I checked the time on my wristwatch. School was almost out. At the entrance to the catwalk I saw a squad car with two police officers seated inside. They looked at me with disinterest, and I walked on toward my bike, which was locked to a fence on the other side of the expressway. I walked the length of the catwalk, hearing the school bell ring across the yard. Then I heard the crack of steel doors opening around the building and the voices of students coming out of classrooms and hallways. I saw kids running across the yard and toward the catwalk, pushing to get in. I leapt out of the way as they set a path for the other side.

There was Desi, from homeroom, also heading to the catwalk. "Hey, Travis, are you coming?"

"What's going on?"

"A rumble."

What he didn't have a chance to say was that this display of violence happened every year. The rules were explicit: If anyone got in the way of the rumble, they'd get jumped. I had not been in class, so I had not heard. I followed Desi, walking my bike at first. We were at the rear of a long line of kids, eager to see what was going on ahead. We had been hooked by our own desire to watch the action unfold. We heard hollers and whistles on the other side of the catwalk. The street alongside the highway was flooded with kids. People filled the road from one side to the other. The police stayed behind while the others walked en masse toward Seventh Avenue. Excited, I mounted my bike and shifted to the lowest gear, pedaling gently alongside the others. Up ahead I saw the gang, walking in a line at the front of the crowd.

"I wouldn't do that," Desi suggested, but I was too curious.

I appeared on a sparkling new Schwinn ten-speed that had been built by my grandfather. I thought I was looking at a break in my struggles. Obliviously, I was slowly coasting ahead between the crowd and the highway when someone grabbed my saddle. I wobbled, trying not to crash. I stood and pedaled faster, trying to get away. But that's when the others saw me and started to converge. Five people were pushing me on my bicycle, running alongside me. Others joined. One grabbed my handlebars, and another grabbed my backpack. I swung a fist, but I hit shoulders. I squeezed my brake levers, but I couldn't stop. They ran me into a mailbox that stood atop a single piece of wrought iron. I flew over the handlebars, over the mailbox, and landed on the dry lawn of some stranger's yard, where I was met on all sides by maroon jumpsuits. They descended on me with punches and kicks.

I curled up into a ball. I was stomped on. I was punched from all sides. Another foot came down, and I took it in the arm. My knees were bent, and my hands were moving fast, catching one fist after another. I saw a small silver blade appear. It came down and forward. I grabbed it. The hand pulled away, cutting my palm. I made a fist of my left hand. I swung, and I kicked and punched until there was no one left to hit. The boys cleared after they saw blood. Then, where I thought another blow would come, I found the sky, and I spun over, hitting the mud.

A crowd approached. I lifted myself to one knee. Students gathered around me, but I didn't care who any of them were anymore. I walked through the crowd, forgetting every face that I saw, promising to never see these people again, not Desi, not anyone. I lifted my bicycle from the wrought-iron mailbox and looked backward toward home. With a wheel bent, I walked. People made way. I saw the assistant principal, but he did not come to my aid. There were teachers who had seen what happened but hadn't helped. The police, still sitting in their car, asked me if I wanted to fill out a statement. I had no answer, and walked past blankly.

There was no way to hide it. I saw the gravity of my situation, and I spoke frankly with my mother about it. We'd come to a dangerous place. After bandaging my hand, and putting ice packs on my head, she tried to think about the future: New World School of the Arts.

"Are you going to do the same piece for your audition?" she asked.

"No, Mom. I'm not getting in with a kids' poem."

"What will you do?"

"Something new, something better," I said.

"Okay. You're the boss," she said gently.

"I'm the boss? Okay, Mom, take me to the bookstore."

At the mall, I found a book of monologues for young actors, and I began flipping through it on the way home. This was the second real book I had ever opened with the intention of reading. It was a thin black paperback with a generic cover and a thin yellow stripe. Inside, each page had a different speech from a play, one serious, the next humorous. Each speech told a story. Not having to think about who the speaker was made the book easier to trust somehow. On one page there was a story about a woman surviving an assault, and on another page there was a story about a mother going to confession. There was one story about a kid who liked to go to the movies all the time. There were no connections between these pieces. None of the characters would ever meet. My arms bruised, my hand wrapped in gauze, I turned the pages, interested to know what character and what part of what play would introduce themselves next.

♦ ♦ ♦

I was standing in the hall, having just swept it, when my mother's voice took me by the ankles and traveled all the way up my neck. Her scream seemed to be coming from every room. I heard the entire chorus of my mother's voice echoing off of the wooden paneling and the broom in my hand.

B.J. had been found in the backseat of a car in Seattle. He'd been dead for eight weeks, nine, and was difficult to identify. The coroner had requested his dental records to verify his name. He had been missing from December 26, 1987, until March 2, 1988. My grandmother told my mom that B.J. had taken a toxic overdose of drugs: alcohol, cocaine, opium, and two different mood stabilizers. The body was received in the coroner's office the day before Grandmother's birthday, March 3. When the news arrived she thought the true story, the full story, wasn't even worth telling. My mother, knowing only what she heard, took the information she received and ran.

"Oh my God, he's finally done it!" She was sure her brother had been depressed, and now she was certain that he, in despair, had given himself a lethal dose. "An *orgy* of drugs," she cried. She kept saying "every pill in the book," like I'd never come to know better. *I didn't read books.*

After the emotions settled, Mom forbade Joe and me from ever speaking of her brother again. It was too hard for her, she said. Joe and I sat in the front seat of his Camaro, rolled down the windows, and turned the radio up.

The date of B.J.'s death was recorded as "1-?-88."

CHAPTER FIFTEEN

The Arlequinade

The fool has a long history. I am certainly not the first. With the fall of the Roman theater, so fell the fool, or the clown, who was until then well adored. The church continued on long past the fall of Rome, its ceremonies preserving some of the theatrical conventions of the older theater. Through religion the theater survived. Though more somber and more serious, the church began to perform the story of the Passion of Christ using theatrical methods that had been developed previously and handed on. Over centuries, these methods became more complex, and more lifelike. Horses drew carriages on which, like floats in a parade, the stages of the Passion were reenacted. These stages roamed the countryside in the Middle Ages, bringing the story to communities that had no access to books and little ability to read them. The Passion plays took the shape of a traveling procession. Like a carefully formed sentence, all of the stages in sequence were drawn out for the people to see.

In the early Italian Renaissance, the theater reemerged by way of companies of traveling actors. Again, clowns fell out of carriages, and the fool was returned to the cities of Italy. Ushering in the Passion play came these Renaissance clowns. To be a clown, or to be made a fool, was no different than to be made a fool of. It meant being someone without legitimacy—someone whose word did not carry weight or convey reliable information. If clowns were paid, it was partly out of pity for their nomadic lives and minimal possessions.

The conventions of the theater were very basic. There were no electric lights or microphones. Actors had to earn their audiences' attention, calling out their lines and moving in stylized ways, to claim the space of the action. They did not rehearse plays as such or use scripts. Over three hundred years they produced theater, and yet only a handful of scenarios, or arguments, remain. These were used as outlines for their performances, which would begin to take place in piazzas all around the Mediterranean.

Every performer was in some way a clown. Masks were worn to individuate their characters and to create an attractive sense of the bizarre. If the action fell apart, each performer had a collection of gags and jokes to draw upon at any time—to earn the attention of his onlookers. Most of the actors were illiterate, and they performed to an illiterate crowd. If anyone in the audience was reading a book, a clown would be likely to pull it out of that person's hand and try to read it upside down as though saying, "Who's the fool now?"

The commedia dell'arte popularized character clowns with names, relationships, even genealogies. Punch and Judy come from this tradition. The clowns Romeo and Juliette come from this tradition. But the most beloved clown in the Renaissance was the child servant Arlequino, a slave taken from his family in Ethiopia. His innocence was what made Arlequino so endearing, but he was more than endearing. Like that of an early Charlie Chaplin, his innocence could be ironic or subversive. He could even be a critic. He was uneducated, untaught, but he was not without his wits or wiles. His naïf humor was understood by all who were acquainted, and it got him into all sorts of trouble. His illiteracy, his lack of education, became the premise of more than one scenario. Arlequino would be sent with letters because he could not read them. Arlequino, was always sincere, was charged with stealing a loaf of bread, even when he had been given it. He was often made the scapegoat, and yet he never doubted his friends. Why would he? His happiness came from the belief that everything he was told was true.

Arlequino suffered, and he knew the whip, but he seemed to have no ability to sense the injury of servitude or his estrangement from family. He had moments of sadness and moments of glee. Had he been assigned by royalty, he'd have been a page. Like a page, he left his home without grief or remorse, and accepted his servitude under Pantalone. He was a fool inasmuch as he now believed himself wealthy. He had horses to feed, and stables to clean. He had friends who loved him and reciprocated his affection for humanity.

One day, Pierrot and Colombina are going to the ball when they find Arlequino cleaning. Children as they are, they wonder why it is that Arlequino was not invited. He doesn't know. The friends find his absence unacceptable, and the scenario then develops around the problem that the servant boy has nothing to wear. The friends gather, and their solution is extraordinary. Each of the children going commits a swatch of his or her gown so that from them an outfit for Arlequino can be fashioned. At the ball, all of the children arrive with diamond shapes cut out of their own garments. At the center of the ball is Arlequino dancing, wearing only the patches he'd been given. This is the origin of the diamond-patterned costume that universally distinguishes this prince of fools.

♦ ♦ ♦

My audition for New World took place on the third floor of a downtown building. I stood in knee-high matching white Converse high-tops bound up tightly with a red lace on the left shoe and a black lace on the right. I wore a pair of green pants, a blue-and-purple plaid shirt, and a colored bandanna on each wrist. I waited in the hall with fifteen other students who were quietly reciting their lines, practicing their gestures, and walking through their auditions. No one talked. We were too nervous. When my name was called from the doorway, I found nine teachers seated along one wall of a small carpeted room. These were my "jurors." I said hello and gave my name. I said I would be playing the part of Stony, from *Marco Polo Sings a Solo*, a play by John Guare. The monologue is absurd, but meaningfully. Stony, who you think must be stoned or at least a bit off his rocker, rants enthusiastically that scientists have had the wrong idea about the intelligence of vegetables. By the end of it, he says that human beings are plants, arguing that:

We are what we grow out of.

The nine jurors looked back at me, coldly. They each had a name tag. "Cindy" looked at "Andy," "Jim" looked at "David." Then "Dr. J" asked me: "Could you please do the piece again? A little slower this time."

I turned, left the room, and walked back up the hallway. When the door closed, I then took a breath and repeated my entrance—this time to some laughter: "Hello, my name is Travis and I will be performing the part of Stony from *Marco Polo Sings a Solo*. . . ." They sat with me through the whole routine again, chuckling. After I was done, there was a little interview. I was asked a few simple questions, like why I had laced my shoes up that way. I said they were lucky I had matched my shoes at all. "I usually don't."

"Fair enough," one teacher said.

Another asked me to tell them about the character I'd been performing.

"Stony? Um, he's one of those guys who are too smart for their own good," I said. "He sees that everything is connected to everything else, and that, for him, is sometimes . . . too much information."

"Too much information?" one teacher laughed.

"But that's who Stony is," I said. "To him, even a flower can be too much information."

After being excused, I heard one of them say: "I like him. He's cute." I was in.

♦ ♦ ♦

Mother came back from Daytona depleted. There had been no funeral. A brief mention was made of Uncle B.J. by a priest where he had been given Communion. Grandmother and Grandfather sat in the pew together. He asked my mother not to make him cry. B.J. was cremated, placed in an urn, and then put away in a closet. B.J.'s death was too much to deal with, and now it was spring. Things were changing. Mother had gotten a new job as an employee counselor at a big telecommunications company. She bought a new wardrobe, did her hair, and decided to quit smoking. She'd always hated cigarettes, she said. From the first puff, she lost all ability to smell. She couldn't tell good meat from rotten meat, and often handed us plates of food to test. When she came home from a twelve-step program bearing flowers she was hoping to catch a hint of their aroma.

When I asked if there had been any news, she said, "Of what?"

"Of B.J.? Does anyone know if he killed himself or not?" I asked rather bluntly. I thought there might have been some investigation.

Mother, surprised by the question, reminded me that there needn't be any more discussion of our uncle B.J.

"Why is that?"

"Kill yourself, that's what you'll get."

"Mom?"

"That's what happens."

In some way, my name would also be taboo that season. When the list of accepted students had first been circulated within the school system—I would learn this much later—my former acting coach from Norland called the offices of New World School of the Arts and raised her concern. "You cannot be accepting Travis Culley," she said. "It really wouldn't be good for the school." According to her description, I was unruly, undisciplined, and a constant source of distraction. She said I'd only be a troublemaker.

The administrator who received the call explained that she would have had to be on the selection committee to influence the names on the list. She was not on that committee, and therefore she could not influence their decisions. The list was published with no changes.

On the day of orientation at New World, I rode the city bus downtown. I arrived early and took a seat in the back of the auditorium. I worried I would be surrounded by strangers. Then I saw Elaini and Valerie from the bus ride to Norland. There was Avi, Bruce, Adam, even Elida and Claudia, the dancers who'd performed with the juggling troupe, traveling from school to school with me in the seventh grade. These were my friends, all of whom I had missed dearly. I ran to them. I was a bit taller, darker, my hair was longer, but I was embraced by my friends as the same innocent page I used to be.

New World was located in the heart of downtown, spread out among seven or eight different buildings on Second Street and First Avenue. Our academic classes took place in the buildings of a partnering institution, Miami Dade Community College. The theater department was located with the music department inside an old bank building off campus. The dance department had studios in a warehouse across the street. The art department was in a vacant Chinese restaurant. In this odd arrangement of buildings I had access to some of the best art and academic teachers in the school system. We'd been brought together from all over the county to share our skills, to discover the potential of our collaboration, and to develop our talents in this unique conservatory training program.

At New World we could say what we wanted, do what we wanted, and imagine the reality of anything we could dream. In exchange, we would have to be committed to developing in our chosen disciplines. I had to be willing to be at school from early in the morning until late at night, attending rehearsals and performances. There were few breaks, no sports, and little rest. This would be the case for all students, and it was the only realistic strategy for success. The reverse was also true: the surest chance of failure belonged to that student who, for behavioral or academic reasons, showed a wavering commitment. I could be cut for having anything below a C average. I could be cut for excessive absences. I could be cut by the theater department if I did not maintain a standard of excellence or show some growth throughout the year. In each department, there would be juries at which we were expected to perform at our highest level in front of a board of our teachers. This was when our progress would be formally measured. Barbara Anders, one of our two school counselors, was blunt. She knew what a thin line there was between being original and being "a problem." Our very existence as students here would hinge upon how we would navigate this "slippery slope."

To support our originality, and to give us seriousness as students, we were given no dress codes and no bells between classes. There would be no more hall passes, *ever*! As students, we would be essentially set free. Sylvan Seidenman, the other counselor, spoke up about the meaning of "freedom" in this context. "You come to class if, every day, you think you belong in this environment and you want this chance." Alan Weiss, the principal, said that we would need to help keep the school's image healthy and focused. We were in a "fishbowl," he said, and "everyone was watching." He and Richard Klein had built New World on the model of the LaGuardia High School of Music & Art and Performing Arts.

I came home vindicated. Before my mother and brother, before my father too when we'd visit him, I had accomplished the impossible. By all accounts, my method worked. One way or another, I had gone from being an illiterate nobody to being one of the luckiest kids in the nation.

I returned to Thomas Jefferson, eager to tell my friends about my *new* school, but Gene-John's desk was empty. Over lunch, Ray told me. Again, he'd been outnumbered. This time Gene-John had been leaving school. As the door locked behind him, four older kids trespassing on the property cornered him by the doors of the administration hall and started taunting. Their slaps turned into punches. Gene-John knocked on the doors for help, while the others tried to wrestle him to the ground. He shook them off and started pounding at the little window in the metal doorframe. In three punches, he cracked the window, shattering the glass, and began bending out the metal screen. With one arm inside, he found the breakaway bar and pulled the door open, shouting for help. The doors of the administration offices locked one after another all the way down to the library.

"Why won't you help me?" he cried, as the outsiders followed him in, fists clenched and swinging. Gene-John did not swing back. Instead he put his hand through the safety glass of the red box on the wall and took hold of the fire extinguisher. By the end of the fight, all four were running away from the schoolyard, but Gene-John kept swinging, throwing the cold cylinder at the fluorescent lights that hung in the ceiling, shattering the plastic diffuser and exploding the bulbs. He continued down the hallway, wrecking everything he could with the red tank until there were no lights, only white fumes billowing out of the doorways. I saw the wreckage, and I finished the year wearing black high-tops, talking to nobody.

♦ ♦ ♦

New World's first official day of school was like a festival. I walked through the busy crosswalks and navigated the sidewalks speckled with working people, traffic cops, and homeless people. Then I was surrounded by artists, kids with blue and purple hair, denim jeans pinned together with safety pins, striped and brightly colored socks and shoes. A mohawk walked through the crowd. Skirts, shorts, and tank tops gathered around the entranceway. There were musicians who looked like artists, artists who looked like actors, actors who looked like dancers, and dancers who looked like musicians. Of the four hundred students who began the program, each was unique in some way.

Immediately, I knew this was a place that did more than take learning seriously. It was developing new pedagogies. The teachers saw each student as a future educator, or as someone like themselves who would be able to create lasting works of art. The teachers understood this power. Many of them were professional artists themselves. Even the academic teachers were creative people. They had been chosen from all across the district, like the students had. The curse of Mr. Orsini had finally, and completely, been lifted.

Now, I met Mrs. Leone. She talked about the meaning of found work, the inescapability of childhood as a subject, and even the shapes of books. At one point, Mrs. Leone showed us what a book was. There was a problem: most of the books in class had been written in already. She borrowed a sketchbook from Guy Samuels and opened it to a blank page. She held the book by its spine. "See this? If you imagine yourself standing here on one side of the page and you look across the fold to the other side of the page, you see the day coming." She took hold of one piece of paper and demonstrated by flipping the page. "The next day you stand in the same position you were in, and you see the day coming. Every day is like every other." She kept turning pages. "The book was built as a calendar to explain the passing of days, how it is that the sun passes over the plate of the earth. Any planet in our solar system passes over the earth this way, so anyone can read a book as though planning on a future event or horizon."

Like Mrs. Leone, many teachers would allow us to turn in our assignments in creative formats, and, because of this, I could pass as an average student, whatever *average* meant here.

Between classes, students would gather into small groups, free-styling, imitating our teachers, or performing musical numbers. In the afternoon, a parade of clowns, we went to our acting classes to have all those charms met with critique.

It was difficult to hide my fear of reading from my acting teachers. They were training us to take a piece of writing and translate every word of it into action. They saw behind the process. In every way, the theater was a threshold for learning literacy because it depended upon a full and exact understanding of actions.

In Cindy Gold's class we were to choose a sonnet by William Shakespeare and memorize it. She handed out long pieces of paper on which sonnets had been formatted so that each was about the size of a cookie. I clung to this paper, curious about these poems that I could see and investigate all in the blink of an eye. Cindy said, "Acting is more than reading. Acting is about unlocking the meaning behind words, and sometimes that means choosing. Make a choice, and don't hold back."

Ellen Davis, in her infinite humor, sashayed about the classroom with a scarf, reciting Hamlet's soliloquy to the actors. She was our voice teacher and had a kind of immortality born from the fact that, in the arts, people who have been through very difficult times often thrive. Ellen was a survivor of the Holocaust, and in class she was sprightly, charming, and totally irreverent.

She showed up one day in a poppy-red dress and red shoes, which bore a remarkable likeness to the poppy red of our plastic chairs and the color of one wall. She danced around the middle of the room, illustrating how easy it is to be theatrical if you are aware of your environment. She stood back. "Don't I look wonderful?" We cheered. "If you are talented or not, if you are beautiful or if you are disgusting, one choice is all it takes to be theatrical."

In Ellen's class, we all waltzed about talking to each other with excessive diction. It was infectious, really. Soon, classmates began calling each other "good fellow" and "Syrah!"

"To the latrine, my fellow!"

"Alack! Thrice forth we go!"

"My kingdom for a toilet!"

"Verily!"

"A toilet! A toilet!"

I leapt, pirouetting through the halls kicking a footbag, a page of Shakespeare crumpled in one hand.

CHAPTER SIXTEEN

The Allegory of the Cave

The first year at New World had been something more than a cornucopia of artistic experiences. Being a student here meant becoming more sophisticated about the nature of conventions. There was always another way to look at things—you simply had to borrow another set of eyes. To hear voices was to have a gift. In a theater lecture by our dean, Jorge Guerra, a Peruvian avant-gardist of international renown, we were told about Plato's allegory of the cave: "Imagine three people sitting in a room with no windows. They've lived there all their lives. . . ." When he got to the part about one person getting up from his chair and walking out of the room, experiencing form and shape for the first time, kids were sitting at the edges of their seats. "Everything was different," he said. "There were whole new dimensions available to perception, to thinking and feeling. There was body, form, a source of all of the voices they'd been hearing in the cave. All of the mysteries had been laid bare."

♦ ♦ ♦

At home, as long as I left on time and returned as expected, it didn't matter what I did at school. With Dad gone, Mom had assumed absolute command. There could be no visitors, no friends in the house, no disobedience. She had gone from being the gentle negotiator to being the sole ruler and enforcer. There was no turning back. She was still in a streak of panic. She wore fret on her face, and cursed my father, telling me at one point that she hoped I would *never* forgive him. She resented being locked into a mortgage with two teenage boys to feed.

I thought she should try to accept the situation; Joe and I weren't that much of a burden these days. We were making our own money. I had gotten a job selling novelty gifts at the mall. Joe had gotten a position at Sears selling televisions. But ten months of traveling between home, school, and our places of work meant cutting back on certain graces. I walked in the door, tatterdemalion, unwilling to share the news of my happy day.

"What have you been doing?"

"Only what I'm supposed to be doing, Mom."

"You're supposed to be home by dinner time."

As my mother and brother were bunkered in, strapped to

their chairs, I felt like I was coming and going from Plato's cave. This was the point when the others turned, heard about the shadows, the colors, and thought the man insane.

At home, I was constantly being questioned. Why did I do this or that? My answers were suspect of irrationality. Joe was always looking for something to tell Mom, and she was always looking for reasonable and unreasonable "behaviors." According to her, if I ever did anything without sufficient reason I was "acting out," exhibiting some neurosis, or worse.

I had to be careful of what I thought in the house. Any thought was punished. Metaphors had always come easy to me, but now, if I chose a metaphor, my mother became suspicious of slippage. She wouldn't find any sense in a comparison I made but seemed to be evaluating my wellness on the basis of that comparison. In the background, she seemed to be taking note of the fact that I compared my mind to a school of fish or that I described coming home as though being locked in a cave.

Metaphors themselves were signs, in her mind, of some misidentification of things. She dropped a beat and stepped out of the action to analyze my meaning.

"A school of fish?"

"Fishbowl," I replied, automatically.

Mother seemed to attend to me closely but coldly. She saw me turning my clothes inside out, painting my shoes, and making drawings of space people who were being burned by acid. She never asked me about any of it. She was now an objective observer, only monitoring. I didn't know what she found so interesting.

Because we'd be moving soon, I went through my box of comic books, reading each one to the very last page. My favorite hero was Daredevil, the blind attorney from Hell's Kitchen. I used to think I was something like him, blind though I could see. I opened up the earliest volume and read it for myself. Then I continued, reading all of the thin graphic novels in sequence. When I was done with these, I looked back at the box and the character of Matt Murdock, and I felt some compassion for him. It was a shock to think about how many other characters tried to take advantage of his inability to see.

♦ ♦ ♦

Mother announced a meeting, the first and the last of its kind. Joe and I were called away from our chores. Once we'd gathered, sitting on the living room floor, Mom began. She said that we would soon be entering the "Dark Years."

She listed the changes that had recently taken place. I had been jumped at school, Joe had been arrested for shoplifting, Dad had beaten me up and moved out. B.J. had committed suicide. But there was good news. Mom had quit smoking and had gotten a new job. I had been accepted into New World School of the Arts, and Joe was soon to graduate from North Miami Senior High School. A lot was happening, but "Dark Years"? Her title seemed melodramatic. Besides, placing a title on a play that had not yet unfolded seemed somehow intentionally confusing. Was she developing some psychological shorthand for denial? I turned away, unsure of my role.

"We are going to make it," she insisted, "if we can only

get through these *Dark Years.*" Then she said she'd be taking back her maiden name. She would no longer be a Culley. She would be a Fox, Paula Jeanette Fox. At that point my brother erupted, feeling that he was losing his mother. "You're not going to do that—you're not allowed to! You are a Culley! You are Paula Fox Culley!" He was usually the restrained one, but now he was inconsolable. "You will be a Culley for the rest of your life!" He didn't look to me for support. When it came to this, I was on her side.

Joe grew small and round-eyed. I thought that, for a person who had read so many books, he'd have more flexibility when it came to changing a name. After all, Fox wasn't her real maiden name either. She had been a Fuchs originally. The Fuchs family came from Germany, and Fuchs was changed to Fox when she went to grade school. I understood by this that names did not have to be attached to any origin. Fuchs could be changed. Fox didn't really mean fox. There was no substance to these ideas, nothing real in them at all.

In the coming week, we left the house a complete mess. No one fought anymore. Nothing was gained by arguing. Mother slept in until ten in the morning, and when she woke up she was another person. She seemed to have set down all of her prior assumptions as though they'd been written out on a little notepad and torn from the glue. She was starting over, she said, in every way possible.

I went to school the last week of class and found myself walking around downtown dreaming about how I could change my life. I imagined that I could make a few simple decisions, and thereby never have to go home again. Then, on campus, I saw a purple flyer, a call for auditions that had been posted for a student production of *Alice in Wonderland*. I thought briefly and wrote my name on the list. If I got a part in the play it would mean a few weeks of rehearsal and one weekend of performances.

The next day I stood before the director, Sean Cutler, a senior from New World's first graduating class. I was ready to leap into a Shakespearean sonnet, but everyone was talking and walking about. Sean kept his hands in his pockets while people stepped, ducked, and reached behind him. The table was covered with lists, open scripts, pencils, and props. There was a key, a clock, a candle, a cookie, a teacup, a bottle, and a deck of cards, all of the pieces necessary to tell the tale. The stage manager was yelling, in whispers, at the assistant director, and the assistant director was clicking something at the stage manager, and the assistant stage manager was complaining to the director, who calmly sat back and smiled. Ashley and Kristin, two girls from my class, were having a kind of pantomimed argument in the middle of all this, exchanging non sequiturs. Ashley started singing "La, la, la, la, la," and Kristin began stamping her feet and clapping as though she were a puppet.

"Who's next?" the director asked.

I was standing in the light. "I am." I smiled, looking out.

"And who are you?"

"My name is Travis."

"What will you be doing, Travis?"

"A poem by—"

"A poem?" I was interrupted. The director started flipping through the papers on the table. "Can you read any poem?" He was just being cute, but then he handed me a sheet of paper. "Why don't you try to read this poem?"

"I've never seen it before."

"That's okay." Then in a clownish voice, he added: "We've never heard it before!" The room laughed.

I lifted the paper up before my eyes and the laughter quieted. I began: " 'Jabberwocky' by Lewis Carroll." A beam of light fell on the stanzas, and I read each of the words off the page as though I'd written them. I found the lines, a rhythm, a voice. I felt clues to the right emphasis as I came upon turns in the next stanzas. Albeit absurd, the poem arranged itself—if I played with it—into a crisp sequence of sentences. The words spoke themselves. Each came out clearly. When my minute was over, and the poem was done, I stood back with the other cast members, now quite perplexed, reflecting. Then, like stamping the back of a check, the director thanked me in a big voice and told me to look at the callboard in the coming days.

I left the stage tingling and went outside to walk off my nerves and to let my mind adjust. *How did I do that?* I wondered. *I didn't even know the words!* Somewhat confused, and partly delighted, I spent the next hour in the courtyard kicking a footbag with my buddy Jorge from the music department.

We got to talking about how the world changes quickly, like all the time. "Change takes place before anyone gets to talking about it," he said.

"You mean change lends itself to people?"

"I guess," he said, and kicked.

"I know what you mean," I assured him. "You mean that people only get to talking about changes when they've already taken place, when it's safe to talk about them! Then, words come easily."

Jorge laughed and passed to me. He didn't know what he meant anymore. By the end of our sophomore year we'd developed an amicable friendship. He was a sincere guy, and a talented musician. I found him interesting because English and Spanish were identical in his mind. He saw them both for their values. All the while, he knew Chopin, Liszt, Rachmaninoff. His brain was like an endless stream of information. Jorge denied it. He said that he'd only begun playing piano six months before his audition at New World. I could relate. But when he sat down at the piano, he was a perpetual source of new examples. Jorge was an excellent student, and he encouraged me to do my best in school—to see the importance of the training. "Man, look around you. All of this is going to disappear faster than you know." He was frank with me because he knew: New World was all I had.

Seeing my name on the cast list of *Alice in Wonderland,* I went to the office of the theater department to pick up my script. Sean welcomed me and sat me down. If I took the part he was offering, the whole play would rest on my shoulders. If I was ready to accept, I would be cast as Lewis Carroll, the author, and I would narrate the entire story of Alice start to finish, introducing each of the acting scenes. If I did not want the challenge, or could not commit completely to doing it, he would cast me in a lesser part, maybe as the Dodo.

I accepted the part of the author and agreed to memorize every word of the script. Sean handed me the play. I started cramming as soon as I could, excited about the prospect of really acting. While reading the script, I found it hard to stay in one place. I read some of the opening poem, then I stood and sat down on the other side of the room, laying the book on my desk. There, I read a few more lines. If I sat anywhere too long, I needed to change my perspective. I held the pages up. I pressed them against the wall. I laid them on the floor and spoke the lines to our cat, Princess, under the bed.

> Alice! a childish story take,
> And with a gentle hand,
> Lay it where Childhood's dreams are twined
> In Memory's mystic band,
> Like pilgrim's wither'd wreath of flowers
> Pluck'd in a far-off land.

More than a dictionary, to get a full sense of the work, I needed the original text. At the library, on a sale rack, I grabbed the Penguin edition of *Alice's Adventures in Wonderland* and I began comparing the book to the play. They were different. I read them both through. Most of the lines of the play were the same, or very nearly like the book, but whole sections had been cut. There was no Tweedledee or Tweedledum, no Mock Turtle, no Lobster Quadrille. I did begin to take some pleasure in this process of finding the story behind the story. When I came upon new characters, I wrote their names down on a separate piece of paper. As names gathered in my hand, I began to hear them in my head. A voice was assigned to each. This wasn't crazy, this was how I came to learn to read.

When I grew weary, which did not take long, I rubbed my eyes and returned to the idea that I was only reading a comic book. Imagining the letters dancing made the process easier. Instead of accepting at face value the words I knew, I imagined that I did not know them. Now they came fresh to mind, as though necessary. I saw each word as though it were spoken from a stage, and still I expected to misunderstand the central message. *Was this notion of meaning only there to provoke?* Half-uttered expressions stood up between the pages in my hand. I stopped and covered my eyes—hearing all the possibilities.

♦ ♦ ♦

At the first rehearsal for *Alice*, Sean had us all sit around a table. "So that you know, not everything in this play makes sense," he said. He eyed us. "We are going to have to learn how to make sense of that which, by the nature of the work, is not going to make sense. This is an absurdist masterpiece, and a classic piece of literature, because it presents an image of the imagination that is so true, and so honest, that it has stood the test of time. Other writers cannot seem to do this better. People, like ourselves, keep coming back to the original because it is delightful, and because it helps us understand so many of the conundrums of youth. This is why we are adapting the play for the theater.

"Who knows anything? What is big, what is small? Who is worth listening to, the Caterpillar or the Mad Hatter? The Red Queen or the Cheshire Cat? What is time? And, different from time, what is the hurry that the White Rabbit is in? All these simple questions will appear to Alice to have their own contradictory answers. This is the magic that we will conjure here. Big will seem small, small will look big, the beginning will be very much like the end, and, in a sense, nothing will happen here. Our objective will be as follows: to have as much fun as possible between opening night and the time we strike the set."

The cast looked back and forth at each other cheerfully. "Shall we begin the reading?" Sean asked, deferring, with a look, to me.

Rehearsals took place in the black box theater between four and six, every evening. Ashley, our Alice, flew through every scene. Marc Ostrick was given the part of the Dodo. Jay Krajewski was our Cheshire Cat. The cast had chemistry, and Sean was very good about encouraging us to collaborate. I announced each scene, describing who would come in and out. The cast waited for me as I continued plodding, sometimes, through the lines. Sean often corrected me on the pronunciations of words but I was never asked to speed up, or hurry along. Only if I was patient would the right words come.

By the dress rehearsal, the cast needed no direction. I would set up the scene and Ashley would leap into the next outrageous dilemma in Wonderland. An artist constructed an elaborate tunnel, a five-foot hole through which the audience was expected to enter the theater. I appeared on opening night with a candle and introduced the cast carefully, telling the story of young Alice.

At the end of the show, Ashley joked: "It's not easy, losing your innocence every night."

CHAPTER SEVENTEEN

Crazy for You

My confidence reading, held in secret, now led me to reflect more carefully on the changes that were taking place at home. Mom was keeping track of things a little differently. She muttered that the divorce had not gone as planned while she organized our lives into a little filing cabinet.

Soon we were moving, and our lives were in disarray. Our pictures were packed into a cedar chest. Joe's books were packed away into boxes. I packed my juggler and removed my masks from the wall. These reminded me of when I met Uncle B.J., the moment I first knew that I didn't know *anything*. I packed my spare high-tops into their old shoe boxes. In one of them, I found a crumpled sheet of paper, my first attempt at writing; Easter Sunday, of all ironies. I smoothed the edges of the paper out on my desk. Then I drew the old can of Barbasol from my desk drawer and I set it on top. For a moment, I sat with these two precious objects juxtaposed. Then, when I heard Joe coming down the hall, lumbering like Dad did, I crumpled the letter up again and threw the can into a box.

When I got home from work one night, Mom told me that Gil had phoned her and said obscene things in a prank call. I couldn't believe her, but she insisted. "How did you know it was him?" I asked.

"How do you know it *wasn't* him?"

I didn't believe a word she said anymore.

On the Fourth of July, we didn't celebrate. We had no barbecue, no fireworks, no races. Instead, we moved into a small three-bedroom condominium in a complex called Walden Pond on the very northern boundary of Dade County, and we moved all of our secrets in. In the hallway, Mom hung up the school photos of Joe and me. There were no family pictures except one: a stiff family portrait taken in 1974. I was a one-year-old with a tuft of hair and big round cheeks. The portrait was so old, and in it I was so young, that I could hardly recognize myself.

Our new home was a squat flat in a building that had eight identical units. There was no backyard. We lived in a corner unit, and our kitchen sat near the bank of a rectangular lake. Mom enjoyed the fact that she could look out of our kitchen window and see the water. It didn't matter to her, the shape. Even if the lake had been dug out by tractors, she found the water soothing. She didn't miss the exotic trees or the gentle wind through the schefflera leaves. She was happy to watch the light off the water while she was unloading the dishwasher.

Mother chose this spot for a number of reasons. It was the right price, and it was as far north as we could go without legally leaving Dade County. She worked in Fort Lauderdale, and so the farther north we moved, the closer we'd be to her work. She chose County Line Road because if we had moved outside Dade County, even by one street, I could no longer take classes at New World. She didn't want to risk my place, she assured me, but then I could see that she was giving me a thin line to walk.

Joe was given the corner room, overlooking the parking lot. He didn't complain. I was appointed a small square room with one narrow window and a door. It had a gaudy hutch that had served as a liquor cabinet for the previous tenants. The hutch had a counter, glass shelving, and mirrors on all sides. I used the shelves to keep my extra cassette tapes and comic books. I left my crumpled letter from Easter Sunday out in the open where anyone could see it. The letter, whose paper was now soft like silk, had to be carefully peeled open to be read, and no one did. I was also given a matching set of dressers, one large and one small, and a waterbed that I never got used to. Sometimes I would rather have slept on the floor, but there wasn't room. I turned, feeling the plastic mattress against my cheek, desperately wanting to fall into Neutral.

♦ ♦ ♦

That year, at the school's first TGIF reception, I met a girl, a new senior in the musical theater department. She was a devastating beauty with dreams of being in Broadway musicals. I was a wild child with an eye for the impossible. We'd gathered on the mezzanine level of the main building, an architectural wonder built in the modern style. The party was held on a wide triangular porch that jutted out into a cloudless sky. There was no sign of where we had come from, nothing to orient us, and so we found each other as though without the slightest interference. Her name was Liz. She told me while dancing, but the music blared so loudly, I couldn't even hear myself asking. I met Liz with a series of pantomimed expressions. I was RAFFISH or TRAVIS depending on how close we stood together.

All of my worries seemed to vanish upon meeting Liz Brownlee. She was popular, outgoing, an actress and a singer. After the reception, she invited me to a house party that she was throwing that weekend in Kendall. I went home and begged my mom to borrow her car. I had turned sixteen that summer and had passed my driving test. I asked if I could borrow her new Honda, *only this time,* to go to a school party. Cautiously, she agreed, as long as I got back at a reasonable hour.

I told her not to wait up.

Liz and I spent much of the party talking, and introducing each other to friends we had in different classes. Every word I said seemed to fall into her hands now, and when she spoke I heard her voice as though within me. That night, Liz's house was full of students dancing in and out of the living room. Plastic cups were left spinning on the floor. Colored crepe paper bled into pools of spilled beer, and clothes were abandoned in the pool. I drove home in the early hours of the morning, leaving a kiss on Liz's cheek. I pulled out of her driveway feeling for the first time that I might one day grow up.

The next morning I was awoken with an arsenal of questions: "How late were you out last night?"

"Late, Mom. Not *very* late."

"Were her parents there?"

"Yes. Her mom and stepdad were there."

"Okay. So, let's get this straight," she said, emphasis on every word, "her parents were there and they let you stay at the party until damn near three o'clock in the morning?"

"The party wasn't over."

"Excuse me? Do you expect me to believe that Liz's parents allow her to have parties until three o'clock in the morning?"

"Yes."

"Was there alcohol?"

"Get over it, okay! The only thing that you have to be worried about is whether or not I have a girlfriend."

"You're too young to have a girlfriend," she said, sneering.

"Ha!" I picked up her keys and went for the door. She picked up the phone, threatening to have me arrested.

"On what grounds?" I asked.

"Disobedience."

"I have no reason to obey you, Mother."

I spent the day on the beach with Liz, talking about family. When I got home, the fight continued. My mother threatened to have me committed, hospitalized, sedated. She swore that she would play any card and use her full influence if I ever tried that again.

"Really, Mom? You'd do that for me?"

She was my *legal guardian,* she reminded me, and she could have me locked up for any reason whatsoever. I told her that she couldn't lie to the police, and she couldn't prove to anyone that there was a single thing wrong with me. She was certain there was.

"Did Uncle B.J. commit suicide?"

She stood back, astonished. "He killed himself with drugs and alcohol."

"Was there a note?"

"No. There was no note."

"Was there an investigation?"

"No. Why would there have been an investigation?"

"Do you think B.J. intended to kill himself?"

"You'll have to ask him."

"So you don't know?"

Then something snapped. She started screaming, "Get out! Get out of this house if you don't like it! I'm telling you to leave *now*!" Again, she went for the telephone. She wouldn't say more. Like an avalanche, the situation fell out of hand. I left the house, accusing her of having made up her brother's suicide. It seemed impossible. How could she use the word *suicide* wrong?

Liz advised that I go live with my father.

"That wouldn't work."

"Come live with me!" she said.

In her eyes, I already possessed the confidence to think for myself, and to do what was right. I had my own life to think about, she reminded me. Between Liz and me, she was really the independent one. I was only beginning to understand how she saw the world. Liz was sharp, intellectually, and she was free to do and say whatever she liked at home. Her mother read all her books when Liz was done with them. They piled up like old toys, set down for new ones. Liz wrote me letters. I wrote her poems.

"What should I do?" I asked her.

"Do what you feel is right."

The next day, while talking to Bruce about his new car, I asked him: "Do you think your parents would let me stay at your house tonight?"

"Sure thing, man. They're cool. But why? Like, what's up?"

I told him what my mother had said. "I need a few days, maybe."

"And your brother?"

"He's not on my side."

"Okay." Bruce looked around at the building we'd found ourselves in, a six-story complex with elevators, galleries, auditoriums, and black box theaters. "Is it serious?"

"Yeah, I need a place tonight."

"Sure thing, you can stay at my house. I'm all right. Don't worry. I don't bite." He punched me in the shoulder, and we were both laughing. "You're going to love my car, man, it's a beast I'm telling you! It's a 1966, but it hauls ass, man!" He was trying to cheer me up.

After our classes let out that afternoon, Bruce walked me

to a brown Cutlass Supreme and opened the door for me. There was no paint on the vehicle. It had been paid for in cash and accepted as is, primed in Rust-Oleum. He liked it that way. We hopped in, and, after a few tries, started the engine. The car was great because Bruce loved it; his excitement made up for all of its flaws. With a squeal out of the parking lot, Bruce took to the highway and raced into the heart of rush-hour traffic. When we got to his house on a busy strip of 135th Street, I was welcomed in. Bruce's sisters were as boisterous as he was. Jokes flew across the room. I thought about the stillness and sterility of my own home, and the sour feelings I had to endure there. My house was like a dentist's office compared to Bruce's kitchen. Here there was warmth, laughter, and food enough for everyone.

My third night away from home, two squad cars pulled into Bruce's driveway. Beside them, my mother's Honda pulled up on the lawn. Three sets of headlights glared into the living room. It was late, after eleven, and the police didn't even knock. They stood outside and called me out of the house with a megaphone. Bruce's dad stood behind my shoulder and told me that I didn't have to go. He said I could stay right there if I wanted to. To this day, I wish I had listened to him. Instead, I stepped out of the house and walked right up to the police.

There were two women in uniform, and then there was my mom. All three were giving me the same look. They told me, either I go home with my mother or they would take me to jail. I asked the police to arrest me. I gave them my wrists. I said that I would not go home with my mother unless she'd promise that something would change in our house, and in the way she treated me. We stood there on the lawn waiting for new words to come from the surrounding traffic.

That's when Mom told the police that she was a social worker, and that I was seeing a psychiatrist.

"No I'm not."

"We've been through this."

The police turned to her sympathetically, and didn't hear another word I said.

A minute later I was sitting in the passenger seat of her Honda and she was starting the engine. "Things will change," Mom said, ominously. Voices caved in, sealing my jaws and locking my shoulders. Why did she want me home? I couldn't understand. My thoughts kept running up behind my ears. Pop music filled the car, and, as we got onto the highway, I began quietly hyperventilating. I locked the door. Arriving at Walden Pond, Mother parked the car and opened the driver's-side door.

I didn't move, and couldn't speak. She left me there trying to breathe. I was sealed in glue. I could not stand up. After a few minutes alone in the passenger seat, I found that I could move my wrist and one of my fingers. I slowly opened the door and set my feet on the pavement. When I tried to stand, I fell, knocking my head against the fire hydrant. For a moment, I lay in the parking lot holding my head.

Slowly, I walked past my mother and brother as though they were on display in a window. I locked my bedroom door. Hanging on my wall were the two masks my mother had given me, bonded together as one. I removed the ornament, set it on the counter of the mirrored hutch. With an available hammer, I took aim and shattered it.

Then, with care, I began systematically destroying all of the other breakable objects in my vicinity. I toppled my dresser and smashed my alarm clock. I dropped my bedside table onto a box of old cassette tapes. I broke a tape recorder, pulled the drawers out of my upturned dresser, smashed my lamp on its side, shattered the lightbulb, and kicked the plug across the room. I tore down my drawings and posters. Mother did nothing. No one came to my door. Then I picked up Dad's sixty-pound weights that now sat at the foot of my bed. I looked at myself in the mirrored hutch full of candles, ornaments, and photographs. I lifted the weight to my chest, dropped one foot back, and hurled the bar into the mirrors and glass shelves. I watched my reflection explode into shards. Glass, mirror, plastic, all came back flying, dusting me in the face and arms. The weights bounced and fell to the ground, ringing like a bell.

CHAPTER EIGHTEEN

On Mental Health

It was Friday when I stepped into the lobby of the address in my hand. At the fifth-floor office, I matched the name, Greenbaum, on the door. This test had made me nervous all week. Because of my blowout, Mother had arranged to have me taken out of school for a comprehensive psychological examination that would include the Rorschach test. Inside the office I found a small waiting area with a flowery love seat pushed up against one wall. A lithograph hung above it in a blue frame. I sat down in a pink wicker chair, next to a watercooler, and leafed through a small stack of magazines. After a moment, the office door opened, and an old man in a white lab coat stepped out and introduced himself, chewing and shaking his head. I now understand that he had Parkinson's disease, but at sixteen I found it distracting. The doctor verified my name from a clipboard and thanked me for being on time. I could barely understand him.

Dr. Greenbaum showed me into his office and had me sit down at a small table. "So, how do you feel today?" he said. He asked where I went to school, what grade I was in, and if I liked going to school. I thought he was trying to trick me, and so I gave him one-word answers and watched him as through a mask.

He started asking me simple questions about home, how many brothers or sisters I had. I didn't tell him about my uncle, and I didn't tell him that I had run away after my mom told me to get out of the house. I didn't tell him that my parents had separated after my dad beat me up, or that I had been jumped at school. He didn't ask for specifics. He looked at his watch and began the test.

There were many stages to the exam. He said I should try to think of each section as a game, but that meant they weren't games. We began with an odd deck of cards that didn't have numbers or suits but only shapes, then figures in different situations. I was given flash cards that I had to arrange into a sequence. Then I was given a blank sheet of paper and a pencil and told to draw my family. I drew us all around a huge TV set. I was the shadow in front of the box. He handed me a maze to solve. Then he cleared the table, checked his watch, and told me that he would now be showing me a series of inkblots. As he brought them over, I thought of a branding iron.

The first image was black and white. I told him what I saw: I saw three things. I saw what an average young man would see, I saw what an average young woman would see, and then I saw what I saw. "Where should I begin?" Song voices were harmonizing. Dr. Greenbaum blinked, shook his head, and told me to begin wherever I wanted to. In three equal groupings I began to list what I saw in the first image. "An average young man would see a baseball diamond, the back end of a totaled car, a shaft of light coming into a dark room, pork chops, a squashed bug, a formation of rocks, a continent." I went on. "An average young woman would see a tulip flower, a vagina, a bug, a butterfly woman with two heads on a chariot with two horses, a statue of angels with four falling babies." Then I told him what I saw: "*I* see a four-eyed reptile. *I* see frogs on the bank of a river. *I* see flashlights in a dark pool. *I* see clouds over the Grand Canyon."

Dr. Greenbaum shook his head and showed me the next image. I started right in: "a bird flying into a flower, two unborn babies being pulled from the ocean, a carousel—the saddle and the pole, a hand with a hole in the palm, a brain inside of a stomach, a burn, a birthmark, an arrowhead in a river, a satellite in space, a spaceship, the *Challenger.*"

The next image had color, red and orange, and black. "An autopsy, a pelvis, a slice of the brain, a dog's head swimming in the water, a crocodile, a set of cherubs flying, children falling, a fly in the mouth of an alligator, a series of islands, a centipede, horizons at morning and night, a virus in milk, the shadows of two big birds balancing a butterfly."

"Big birds?"

"Yes, like Big Bird from *Sesame Street,* and they're pouring something into this big brain." I pointed out their hands, their heads, the brain.

The next image began with a train wreck and led to fresh nuclear waste traveling over rocks. The colors in the inkblots were becoming more complex, but they all seemed very intentional, full of angels, animals, insects, bodies, skeletons; people.

In a way it was horrifying. After the last image, a crushed walnut, my eyes were exhausted. Dr. Greenbaum shook his head and tried to catch up with me. I thought he'd be impressed with all of the images that I had come up with. I thought he'd say something like "Very good," but he didn't say anything at all. He turned the pages back one by one, running the butt of his pen down two columns. This time he shook his head for real, flipping back pages until his notebook had finally closed.

I began to feel nervous, like I might have said or done something I didn't want to. I stared at him, trying to tell myself that his shaking head didn't mean anything. In the end, my mother was handed a document that effectively gave her permission to have me sedated and hospitalized at any time she chose.

Dear Mrs. Fox:

Your 16-year old son was seen for a complete battery of psychological tests on October 25, 1989. He was extremely cooperative throughout the testing and worked diligently.

Severe emotional disturbance emerged immediately and was present throughout all test protocols. He has feelings of being left out, of others not paying attention to him, of being different than others, and tends to handle these feelings in a variety of ways that are barely allowing him to cope.

Some of his thoughts are unusual and different. He tends to cover them up with role-playing, but is aware of the fact that some of his percepts are not realistic. Boundaries between what is real and what is make-believe are weak, and at times he responds to his own fantasies as though they were, in fact, reality. This inability to distinguish between his own fantasies and reality places him at serious risk in a number of ways. Should he be a failure in his chosen career of being an actor, he is likely to be overwhelmed by his tenuously controlled inner drives.

In view of his impaired self-esteem and the intense confusion of dealing with sexual feelings, he finds it difficult to approach people of either sex with any intimacy.

He is well aware of his inner conflicts: his working diligently on the test indicated a willingness to work on his own problems. In view of his tenuous hold upon reality, his tendency to act out in aggressive and/or destructive fashions, it may be necessary to hospitalize him at some time during his treatment.

If you have any questions concerning this report, please call on me.

Sincerely,
Richard Greenbaum, PhD

I left the office, and I went to school somewhat by habit, I guess, even curiosity. I didn't have to be there, I felt I belonged. New World was having another of those big TGIF parties. This event, like the last, was equipped with refreshments, a DJ, and something of a dance floor. I didn't want to miss out. The mezzanine was full. People were dancing. Liz was there. I saw Marta by the ledge overlooking the atrium of the Wolfson Building. It seemed all of the theater kids were stressed-out about whether or not they'd been cast in the next main-stage production, *The Suicide*. Then I heard Bruce off in the distance, calling for help, and I thought I knew what to expect.

He'd found a certain detail in the architecture, a second mezzanine protruding from the side of the building. From this, he could stand, raise his arms, and pretend to be hanging off of the ledge. The illusion was successful, and for a second it was funny. In the next second, our health teacher, Dr. Doan, saw Bruce against a blue skyline hanging from one hand, waving the other in the air. She leapt into life-preservation mode, a sixty-year-old marathon runner. When the impulse took, she ran and threw herself against the ledge that Bruce appeared to be hanging from. She grabbed his arms and tried to pull him back onto the mezzanine. Bruce looked up at her from below and turned his hands around, smiling. Dr. Doan grabbed him with both hands, like he was her own child, and screamed.

On Monday, when the call-board was posted, Bruce's name wasn't on the cast list and he wasn't in class. Our new acting coach, Carol Cadby, gave us the news. Bruce had leapt—out of the fishbowl—and was now being sent back to his regional school. It was the worst news a student could bring home. I was devastated. I knew his parents would be crushed. The room felt empty as we came to the end of class. For the first time since coming to New World, we were no more than a handful of listless students wandering through the hallways.

CHAPTER NINETEEN

The Theater of Literacy & Illiteracy

There is a book in my apartment, a book of many volumes. It is a journal, a diary, which I began here in the fall of my junior year and have maintained into my adulthood. The journals themselves vary. They are simple sketchbooks. Most are black or white. There are a few blue volumes, and a set of red volumes. There is one orange journal, and one green journal. They come in some variety of sizes. I have counted them, but as I continue writing, their number grows and I lose track again. Each volume is related to the next, just as each entry is. While the journals follow few conventions, those that I have chosen have come to shape my life.

This is no mystery. If you did any one thing every day, it

would change you much like these books have changed me. It would have to. A new version of yourself would be born of the process you began that day. When I started keeping a journal I didn't know what I was doing, and I never thought the practice, if I maintained it over many years, would turn me into a writer.

Today, I am a published author, a playwright, and an occasional poet. I live in Boulder, Colorado, where I have worked as a bicycle courier and a bookseller. For the last few years, writing has been my focus. Outside of my little apartment, birds and squirrels occupy the trees near the foot of the mountain. As the day passes, and the light in my room changes, these books change too. The weathered spines absorb the light and cast little shadows that mark the time.

When I began this journey, I thought I was an average boy who simply wanted to hold on to his innocence. I wanted to take my time growing up and learn naturally, as I needed to, and in the context of real situations. Art found me. Soon, the plays explained in class would be my new imaginative horizon. The lines were always flexible, with open inferences and intonations. Five actors doing the same monologue could give five different interpretations. This, I have learned, is part of the function of plays. The art of the theater is not to please an audience but to build a structure that can be revealed to one. It requires the actors to breathe through the lines and to express themselves in the work at hand. The theater has less to do with the production of entertainment than with the process of handling a text, and engaging the participation of other people in it. Actors learn their parts, and invent the necessary components of storytelling. The benefit and moral become first absorbed by the producers of the theater. Only then can they be shared.

The same is true with literacy. Writing for yourself, if you develop the discipline, will expedite a learning process. By writing you encounter yourself, and understand your environment. Literacy is a comparative intelligence. It is through comparison that our words become used and drawn upon like currency.

Left to our own devices, we will write about different things. We will use our literacy in different ways. The process is individual to each of us. Describing an event, we will describe it with different words. We speak from where we stand. This is not because some words are right and some are wrong, as I once believed. If this were the case, we would plagiarize each other constantly. By writing, we learn about ourselves. When we learn a new term and begin to expand our vocabulary, it is not by imitation. We do not imitate each other very accurately. It is wrong to think we learn each other's words at all. In truth, we only come to exchange them with our own.

♦ ♦ ♦

Neither Joe nor I had been told. We were given twenty bucks to get out of the house for a while. Mom sent us out to see a film we'd seen before. I don't know how I bought it. I sat in the theater with my brother and I didn't look at the screen. I couldn't watch the movie. Our mother had strapped the images to our faces like blindfolds. By watching, we were being tricked. We were being asked to keep our backs to something, to look the other way.

I thought Mother must be keeping a secret, a lover. I wrote in my journal that she must have a boyfriend. I was right. Years later, she introduced me to the "invisible man" and confessed her reason for covering the relationship up. The problem was not that Joe and I were too young to understand but that she wasn't yet legally divorced.

I would avoid writing this if I could, but I have to be honest about the many levels of deception that were interfering with my view of the everyday world. I could not make easy sense of it all. There were other levels still. The reason the divorce settlement had not been finalized was that Mother was preparing an appeal. While not telling us about the man she would sneak in and out of the condominium, she was preparing to put an argument before a judge that called on supportive documents from Dr. Greenbaum saying that I was psychotic, and might need to be hospitalized.

Her effort didn't work, and the judge denied her appeal. While all this was going on, no one talked to me about any of it. I had not even read Dr. Greenbaum's letter at this time. While my life was being handed around, Mom demanded I stay out of it. The divorce wasn't my business, she said, but that was just something else my mother said. If anything was my business, this was.

Remarkably, while going through the file cabinet, I found out that Joe had gotten there first. He had taken my childhood savings bonds and cashed them with a driver's license he'd forged with his likeness and all of my information. He'd made the license so that if he ever got in trouble driving, I would receive the penalty. Fortunately I discovered it, and I confronted him. It was obvious. My brother had done this because no one listened to anything I said. *Why should he?* He could say I was lying, that I was trying to say I had not spent the money, and no one would believe me. How would I prove him wrong? Because I was illiterate, had been, he still thought he was able to take advantage of me. Even though I could now read and did write, his perception had not changed. To my brother, I was simply a confused person with no sound identity, no memory attached, and no rights worth defending. He could tape any word to my back and I would never be able to refute it.

For safety, if not for pride, I knew I would soon have to be leaving home. It seemed better than being taken advantage of. The idea filled me with anger. I would have to leave my family because lies were now the rule. Leaving home would change the most essential thing about me, my relationship to documents. I would need to keep account of things myself, and record what other people said. I would need to acknowledge my intuition, my feelings about the people I met. I would have to be the keeper of my own archive. *I would only know how the world really worked,* I thought, *once I could find a reliable way to look back on all this mess.*

To start, I would need to establish a separate space to act as an intermediary between two worlds: the world as it was and the world as I saw it. By leaving a few observations in a notepad of some kind, I thought I could make my pen a tool that could continually test and measure my adjustment to "reality." I knew that if I didn't develop the literacy needed to write my story, to tell the truth about what happened, someone else could step in and alter it. I had to find a way of knowing who was lying and who was not lying. Only by writing would I see for myself who spoke the truth. My literacy would be a test, in this sense, to see whose words held true. I envisioned having a book that stayed with me, a constant companion. This would be a journal built on some of the basic conventions of the first. It would not be random, but it would be coded and organized by different-colored inks. Inasmuch as I could plan it, this book would serve many purposes and have multiple, parallel functions. It would keep a record of my thoughts and experiences, documenting important events and the many ideas they led to.

My journal begins on the morning of November 22, 1989. That day, as per our new routine, Mom drove me to the gas station on Route 441 at the corner of Ives Dairy Road. At this anonymous bus stop, I caught the I-95 Express downtown.

"Have a good day, Travie," Mom said through the window. These little goodbyes were rehearsals for the real goodbye we would soon face. I was not a boy any longer. I had knowledge from someplace she could never understand. I still wore my mismatched sneakers and painted-over pants. I wore my hair long, and over my face. I wore a concert shirt, Jimi Hendrix or Jerry Garcia, and always I tried to hide what I was feeling. Even though I did not do drugs, I let people think what they liked.

My mom thought, as all moms do, that dressing the way I did meant that I wanted to be seen by everyone, that I wanted to be the center of attention. She was wrong: I did not wear my hair long to be cool. I didn't wear my jeans tight to be sexy. Since Norland, she'd stopped buying me clothes I would actually wear. She bought me slacks and penny loafers, things that were ridiculous. This was why the jeans I wore eventually developed holes. Now in my junior year, I was still dressing like the juggler from the seventh grade—and in the same digs.

This morning like every morning, Mom pulled into the street and I paced in the darkness behind her like a number sign, dressed like a game of tic-tac-toe. When my bus came and the doors opened, I boarded, showing my monthly pass to the driver. I sat next to the same elderly woman as always and opened a book of sonnets. By the time we saw the margins of downtown, I'd closed my book and pulled the cord to signal for the first stop. I couldn't sit a moment longer. I held my bag by its straps, scurried out the door, and ran the rest of the way to school. I jumped over sewer grates and curbs. I ran alongside the bus and then turned down Second Street, dodging pedestrians. After the first block I felt better, by the second I felt great, and by the time I got to school, eight blocks later, I was ready for anything and early for school.

In Mr. Padgett's class I sat among friends, passing notes with Rita and Chris, from Norland. Today Chris was drawing surreal, amoeba-like cartoon figures, painted like candy canes. Together, we ignored Mr. Padgett. It wasn't that we didn't care about class. On principle, we didn't care about *excelling* in Geometry.

In Biology, I felt like I was changing my skin. It was the formaldehyde. I spent the hour making a list of all the intruding ideas I had that hour and discarded them.

An hour later I went to the church for American History. On a page, I started drawing a disembodied eyeball with one hand holding it in the air, the arm dissolving into the cosmos. Whatever I saw today seemed to stick together and come apart. I remembered my journal from Thomas Jefferson. After the move, I had lost track of it. Now, I felt the itch to write again. I listened and waited with my pen. Voices pointed to objects in the room that were like ciphers, revealing more information behind them as though from behind a seal that I could almost lift the edge of. I needed a book to write in. I scratched my page, unwilling to let this stream of thoughts get past me.

Then it came to me: *make one*. I reached into my backpack and gathered together all of my paper. I was unlacing my right shoe when Mrs. Clarke politely asked, "Mr. Culley, can you explain to the rest of class what you're doing?"

"Me?"

"Yes, Mr. Culley? If you please . . ."

"I'm writing in my journal, Mrs. Clarke."

Kids were chuckling. Mrs. Clarke smiled with them. "Thank you for being honest, Mr. Culley. Pardon me for asking, but why do you feel the need to take off your shoes?"

"The binding."

"Come again?"

"For the binding."

"And have you read the assignment?"

After class, I crossed in the middle of the street, one painted canvas high-top scuffling along loosely behind me. During break I cut the other shoestring in half and tied my high-tops with half laces.

In Mrs. Ledesma's French class, I wrote: *I can't handle today. I've got to get out of here.* The ink from my black felt pen was too thick for my hand. The letters struggled to identify each other. I felt that I was training myself to face certain still unknown realities, and to cope with still unmet emotions. Each entry was then another experiment in reaching the heart of a current predicament. I didn't know what they would eventually lead to, so fragments were as welcome to me as questions. I wanted to see for myself how, among all of the world's reflections, I truly appeared.

The next day, on Thanksgiving, Joe and I sat with our dad in a tacky seafood restaurant eating mussels and shrimp. He had a new mustache. "How are you guys doing in school?" he asked, chewing.

Joe had graduated from high school, with honors, and was thinking about college. He wanted to stay in the area.

"Travie?"

"Next week, I'll be auditioning for a play."

"Really?" Dad took interest, wiping his hands. "What's it called?" He was waiting for something rich.

"The Suicide," I told them, and they both laughed. "No one dies in the play. It's a *farce, you guys."* They laughed louder.

Heading home, I asked Joe if he thought Dad should know about our uncle.

"They're divorced, Trav. Why should he know?" I turned down the radio in his car, reminding him that B.J. had sent him one first. Joe remembered the white box. "You're right. I'm not sure if he knows." We drove. Joe never said I was right about anything.

"I don't think B.J. killed himself." I let the missile fly.

"What are you saying?"

"Well, think about it. Dad had no sensitivity about suicide when I mentioned the name of my play, neither did you. Either he doesn't know, or there was no suicide. Which do you think is more likely?" Joe was trying to pay attention to the road.

"You and I, we are not grieving a suicide, are we?"

Joe hit the brakes hard at the light. He had questions: "Presuming you're right, and B.J. did not commit suicide, who killed him then? How did he die?"

"It was an accident, probably. Mom wants to wrong him for it. She came up with the suicide—to scare us."

"From what, drugs? She wouldn't do that," Joe said, but then he thought again.

"Parents lie to kids, Joe. It's easy: Santa Claus, the Tooth Fairy, the Easter Bunny."

"This is not the Easter Bunny. You're saying she lied to us about B.J. to scare us?" My brother couldn't grasp it. "Why should I believe you?"

"Would you believe her?"

"That is not enough! It doesn't mean that B.J. *didn't* kill himself!" He was pulling his head out of a paradox.

"Joseph"—this was his new nickname—"suicide is something a detective has to prove." Then I reasoned it out: "In a suicide, a detective goes to the scene of the crime and picks up every bit of evidence to rule out the possibility of it being an accident, or—"

"What?"

"Or motivated."

Silence.

"A suicide is intentional, *premeditated*." A voice came to the rescue with all the right words. "Think, Joe. If there was no note, and no sign of an intended death, then why would anyone—without evidence—jump to the conclusion that he killed himself? How does that clear the matter up?"

"You tell me."

"It only clears the matter up if it's a lie." Joe had no reply. "She wants to guard us from turning out anything like him."

He listened, keeping his eyes on the wheel. "Why would she do that?"

"I'll ask."

We pulled into the condo and parked by the hydrant. Mom was alone, sitting in her chair with a glass of wine.

"How is your father?"

"Nice, Mom." I stood there, ignoring the question. Then I asked, "What really happened to Uncle B.J.?" I knew it was rude, but I was angry.

She looked at me, grimly. "Why?"

"Does he know?"

"What do you mean, 'Does he know?' "

"Does Dad know that B.J. committed suicide?"

She stared.

"Was it a suicide?"

"Well, yes," she burst out. "Your uncle, with his own hand, killed himself using dangerous, illegal drugs. Don't you call that a suicide?"

"Wasn't he on medication?"

"Yes. I think he was on medication."

"Do you think he took that with the intention to kill himself too, Mom?"

"Travis, *suicide* is a clinical term. It means causing harm to oneself." I listened. "B.J. caused his own death with drugs that he knew were dangerous. That is, clinically speaking, a suicide. What else do we need to go over?" She kept going around, trying to say the same thing. Then she shifted. "Are you thinking about hurting yourself?" She sipped from her glass, peeking down, ready to draw her ace.

This was, of course, what she spent much of her time doing at work: following up on desperate calls, counseling people in distress, catching them at the moment of breaking. She thought herself a master at handling these sorts of problems.

"No, Mom, being suicidal is a psychological state. It means having the *intent* to die, an interest in dying. I don't want to die. I want to know."

She sat forward and put down her glass. "Okay, I'm done. If you're not at risk of hurting yourself then I don't know why we're talking about this. Happy Thanksgiving."

The next night, she hid in her bedroom, curled up on the right side of the waterbed, staring blankly into the glow of some news channel. Needing confirmation, I went into her room. I left the door cracked and I turned off the TV set. Mother sat up and howled. Our fight raged.

She ordered me to turn on the TV, and I ordered her to tell me the truth. She threatened to have me committed, and I threatened to run away. She said she would call the police and have me hauled away for disruption. I said I'd have her hauled away for—

"For what?"

"For breaking your oath."

"*What* oath?"

♦ ♦ ♦

After the long weekend, as I walked down the hall at New World, my classmates started to congratulate me. One after another, art and music students were saying "Good job" and "Congratulations." Both Liz and I were among the students to be cast in *The Suicide*.

Liz was offered the lead female part, acting across from Jay, our once Cheshire Cat. I was cast as the butcher, Pugachev. I had only three lines, all comedic. I walked onstage with a five o'clock shadow that I applied myself and a bloody apron. In the glow of the theater lights, Liz, in a white wig, knew every beat. When she needed a cue there was another actor ready with it. The script we'd rehearsed so many times seemed to completely disappear between the actors. This incredible instructive illusion, this force of coordination, was magical because at the end of the night it led me back to myself. Liz and I took off our makeup in the same mirror, setting ourselves aside from the illusions of our characters.

CHAPTER TWENTY

Epiphany Junkie

Tears for Fears came to the Miami Arena in the summer of 1990. I had spent four weeks that summer in Kansas, at Lovewell, a young creative arts workshop that I attended with fifteen other New World students. Looking forward to my return, Liz bought two tickets for the concert. When I came home, I told my mom why I needed to borrow her car that Friday night.

"Absolutely not."

"Liz already bought tickets, Mom."

"I don't care," she said, unaffected.

"Well, that's great, Mom."

"Shut up. You know, save it. You've had your fun."

The truth was that she had already booked me for a doctor's appointment on the same Friday. She told me I was being tested for a chemical imbalance, but then this wasn't true either. When the doctor read from her report that there were no drugs in my sample, I realized: Mom had only thought I was high.

To make matters even worse, on this visit, I was prescribed a tranquilizer—a "mood stabilizer." Like it or not, I was *another* B.J.

I argued against it. I didn't want to take drugs. I said I didn't *need* drugs, and got upset about it. Mom began to point to my agitation as the reason for them. "Don't you want to have better control of your emotions?" She was being patronizing. "Try it. See how it feels." What she was presuming was such an insult that I could not express my anger. Truth was, my being sedated would only make her more comfortable.

Mother said it was mandatory. I *had* to take the drugs, so I did. I took one pill with a glass of water and slept for three days. I fell into dreams that dovetailed into other dreams indefinitely. I went from one world to another like I was falling backward down a set of stairs. I slept until I didn't know if I was thinking or dreaming, or just coming up with new things to do in this vast, unformed space where anything could appear or disappear, a place in which all things, once forgotten, again became easily available. I slept through the Tears for Fears concert, but as groggy as I was I couldn't leave the house anyway.

Bruce was grateful for the ticket. He picked up Liz in his 1966 Cutlass Supreme, and they had a great time. What else are good friends for?

I stayed home, dreary, seated on my waterbed as though on a magic carpet ride, when it dawned on me: *I had no reason to fear my own thoughts.* I wasn't crazy. I didn't have a chemical imbalance. I remembered the purpose of my journal, the original purpose: to account for my own feelings, to know them, to be able to own them, and yet, in this awkward moment of my life, I wasn't so sure of what I was feeling. Irritated, aching from too much sleep, I grabbed my old journal and I saw right through the pages in my hand.

I thought about the thickness of the pages, and I remembered what Mrs. Leone had said about books. I leafed through the unused pages before me, and I knew they meant a future. No matter the obstacles ahead, there would be pages to recount exactly how I passed through them.

Finishing the first page of a third journal, I could be confident. There were days ahead, and days behind. I would have the ability to think, to write, and to express myself every day of my life, even the last.

The next batch of pharmaceuticals was gentler, I thought, but my view was still obscured. It felt like mood swings, but in truth I think I was open, susceptible to suggestion. I went with my environment, meandering down sidewalks as though I were the first pure consciousness to perceive them.

Even with the new drugs, I could seem to access the voices in my head easily. They walked with me. Like with a radio receiver, I could tune in to this voice or that. I could turn voices into music simply by providing them with a few instruments and assigning them positions in the band. Some were available only for counsel. Some would never play.

♦ ♦ ♦

My senior year began in a state of high anxiety. Liz had flown off to Otterbein University only three days before school began. I was a wreck about this. She'd left me here with all of my troubles. We couldn't be sure if we'd ever see each other again. She knew that my concerns were too immediate, my focus too close at hand to expect lengthy reminiscent letters. I was about to begin my last year of high school, and I could hardly think through all the changes that were taking place.

Juries had been scheduled for the second week of the year. I had four monologues to prepare. My eyes were saturated with the lines of characters. My head was full of my mother's new antidepressants.

On Friday, September 7, 1990, I was awoken by the voice of Henry the Fifth, doing "Once more unto the breach . . ." I drove to school in a boxy hand-me-down Chevrolet that my dad's mother had passed down. The car was supposed to be for me exclusively, but Joe's Camaro had died, no surprise, and now he and I were expected to be sharing this, driving each other places. We'd fought endlessly that summer about who deserved to drive and who didn't.

It was a flat gold 1980 Caprice Classic with four doors and dome hubcaps. I kept the windows down, blasting Nirvana.

I have a number of entries from this day, and a number that would follow *about* this day. It was the moment in which everything really did seem to change. I describe having a headache. I imagined I had a marble, glass, implanted deep in my forehead. It was dense like a planet, and consumed by storms. To this planet, all other things were held in orbit. This could have been a side effect of the drugs I was taking—dizziness, nausea, dry mouth—but I was also at a peak of exhaustion. All of my voices seemed to be calling to the planet in my head, something like wolves to the moon. As I drove to school, I felt my body swirling. This magnet was pulling together the space between my eyes. I parked in the student parking lot and found the atrium of the new building on Northeast Second Street. I was home again, but I felt like I was in terrible danger.

Today, New World was celebrating the grand opening of its new building. Everywhere there were decorations and cheer. The nine-story building had glass blocks and yellow external stairways. The façade was a pink awning with a fat yellow pillar in the middle, nothing like the WPA-style mortuary where my story began. From the lobby, I stepped into an elevator that quickly became crowded with students from the school's various disciplines. Some I knew and some I didn't, but standing close to me were painters, musicians, dancers, and actors, all of whom were filled with excitement. That morning, I wasn't one of them. I was a mix of emotional exhaustion, fascination, and panic.

In the building, each floor had been designated for a different purpose. Academic classes were held on the second, third, and fourth floors, administration was done on the fifth and sixth floors, dance on the seventh. The eighth floor housed a dance studio and two large performance spaces.

The ninth floor was equipped with offices, a design shop, two movement rooms, a lighting lab, and three acting studios.

Because I'd failed Mrs. Clarke's class, I was starting this year on academic probation. I could have no electives outside of my arts classes. For first-period American History and second-period Government, I was in the same room. Mr. Suarez was my teacher for both hours. After Government, I went one room over to Mr. Wimmers's for Philosophy, and I delighted in the fact that I could take a course in "thinking."

Mr. Wimmers was a more handsome Jean-Paul Sartre, and an encyclopedia of jokes. His lectures attempted to act as an overview of philosophy, but then, "What is philosophy?" he asked us. The discussion was always open.

There was no doubt, all of this thinking took place in language, but Mr. Wimmers asked, "What is language?"

Materials were assigned for every week of class, but he said frankly that we didn't have to read them. "If they don't interest you, don't read them. If they *do* interest you, you're welcome to look into them. We'll discuss all of the ideas in class." He began talking about Skepticism and Stoicism, then the difference between Sophism and Cynicism. He described Diogenes, the cur, who lived in a wine cask.

After fourth period, Science, I had lunch with Jorge Mejia and John Emerson in the parking lot. We found the hood and roof of my car to be sturdy enough to handle the weight of all three of us. I told Jorge about the headache that I was having.

"What does it feel like?"

"Not good." I could actually see through this planet,

which seemed to bend my vision. In moments, I could see through things: oceans, hurried cloud formations, passing under my skin. I leaned back on the hood of the car and held my head, but the pain would not go away. Jorge and John were talking about some inquisition story in a book they were reading in AP English.

I looked off at the people coming up and down Second Street, alongside the old Cuban church. I saw a woman walking up the sidewalk, and then she was transparent. I saw through her: *solids, liquids, and gases.* By their arrangement, and in how she held them, or mixed them, I could see how this woman felt, where her thoughts were aimed. Voices emerged, in song this time, as the noon church bells rang.

Everyone was running. In my eyes, one person appeared to be filled with a pale liquid, their limbs solid like blocks. In another, I saw shoulders and crown spinning in a light gaseous cloud. They were lost. It must have been the drugs, I thought, causing this peculiar transparency. I pointed to my third eye and asked for aspirin. The next person to come into view was a businessman in a light gray jacket, brown leather shoes, striped shirt, and pants that fit him imperfectly. He seemed to be an uncomfortable assortment of corporate formalities. He looked at us, and looked away. Without the time or the space to acknowledge us, he seemed to consider us of little importance. Right then, I could see through him. He had one half of a solid head, and a rigid back. His face was full of worry, and he seemed to float with every step he took. From the waist down, he was mixed up and gaseous. He didn't know where his feet were going. To me, it seemed his stare was made out of a small collection of rocks. I rubbed the marble, having finally attained *super-vision.*

"So Alyosha is right," Jorge advanced.

"No, Ivan is right," John objected.

"Does God suffer when children become the victims of injustice?" Jorge asked.

"There is no God," John said, quoting the character Ivan.

"Yes, but God doesn't know that," Jorge mused. "He only *thinks* that."

God doesn't suffer. He doesn't feel anything, I thought to myself.

I kept watching people, and I realized that if other people were constituted as I saw them, then I was constituted as they saw me. I imagined how I could begin to direct the constitutions of people, strangers or anyone, like I was directing a play. I could change their internal makeup by drawing or repelling their attention. Knowing my constitution as a performer, and their constitution as receivers, I could draw them wherever I wished by setting heavier things in place, like channeling water. Gas could only be captured or lost. Solids grew imperceptibly. I thought I could simply open a window in my mind and make other people look out of it.

Then it was time for class. I sat up and got my book bag. We took our separate paths. As I walked, a radio was on in a nearby storefront, and from it a voice emerged: "Travis." I turned around. No one was behind me. But whose voice was this? I recognized it. Was someone playing a trick on me? Then, Marta turned the corner, giving me every sign of recognition. She strutted up beside me with a cigarette.

"Marta, did you just call my name?"

"No."

"You didn't?"

"Are you hearing things?"

"It's *Vance* I'm hearing."

"Who?"

"He taught me how to crack my knuckles in the third grade."

"Are you *okay*?"

I wasn't sure. I felt like my feet were swinging in place, my toes dangling above the sidewalk. She looked me right in the eye and double-checked me like I was high. "C'mon, I'll walk you."

I spent five minutes in the third-floor hallway drinking from a water fountain and tasting nothing. When I came into English, with Mr. Remis, I was already late. He shook his hair at me and had me sit down. Remis was something of a flamboyant guy, but it was only a pretense. I found him to be a construction of imbalanced stereotypes. He wore wooden clogs, a scarf, and a thin belt. He maintained his curls to match his mustache and beard. He lingered on ambiguous words like *pet* and *ought. Litra-ture*—he said these words like they were his special domain. I wrote out my unraveling thoughts. I let my hair hang over my eyes and kept my nose in my journal.

In the afternoon, the elevator opened onto the ninth floor, and a pack of theater students emerged: Marta, Dacyl, Adam, Valerie, Marc, and me. We walked into a freshly painted hall with polished marble floors and new lockers. The studio was complete with new lighting equipment, curtains, and wooden floors. The space was divided into an acting area and an audience area, and today, we were the first senior class in the building. We assembled for a special seminar called the Forum. Most of the kids sat in cushioned chairs that had been set about haphazardly.

Once the room had filled with students, the associate dean, Dr. Richard Janaro, came in and gave us a little slapstick. Before he began he seemed to forget his big surprise. He gave a wink and went back to the door as though to close it, but he couldn't close the door without dropping his folder. The latches didn't make sense. "Could you hold my folder?" he asked Avi, but he handed Avi a set of keys. They traded the keys for the folder. While our teacher thumbed the keys, the door closed—leaving him in the hall. We heard a knock on the door. It was Dr. J.

Avi gave him the folder and he proceeded to center stage, drew a page from his folder, and began. "Is this the right room?" There was laughter. We gave him a little round of applause. "As you can see on your schedule, every Friday we will be holding forum here in this room. Think of it as an hour, outside of whatever else is going on, to come together to talk. We will be summing up the events of the week, processing what we have gone through together, and getting news about what will be happening next. This is your hour. You will be able to set the agenda and ask whatever questions you like. I don't claim to know much, but I'll give you the best answers I have." He looked down at a few notes scribbled on the outside of his folder and reset the spectacles on his nose.

"Did you bring your journals? Every student will need

one. The journal is for the forum, and the forum is for you. There is no right or wrong way to participate, except if you do not participate, *understand*?

"I will be collecting whatever you want to write throughout the year. It can be for me or to me. It can be anything you like. Don't view the journal like it is an assignment. *It is mandatory,* but nothing will be judged or graded. I will make a few general comments in the margins and then hand them back. There are no grades for this course, but you'll never have another class like it. You are the subject of this class. That is what is meant by *forum.* You are being heard, so please try to show up."

Dr. J began with a discussion about how we saw ourselves in the theater, and what we could expect looking forward from here. Students spoke their minds. Some wanted to be famous, others wanted to be playful. A few students spoke to wanting to find themselves. Some students admitted wanting to be other people, some felt trapped in this life, in what they were. I leaned up next to Marta, and pressed my hand to my forehead.

CHAPTER TWENTY-ONE

Emancipation

The next antidepressant made me all warm and fuzzy. They were these little pills and they were coated in a sweet hospital-green coating. "These are good! Are they placebos?"

"Of course they're not."

"But they're sweet, you should try one."

"Come on."

Nothing softened my arguments with Mom. I wanted out of the house in which there was neither sanity nor freedom. She said that I was too crazy to be trusted on my own.

I scoffed.

Then, only three weeks into my senior year, I got the signal that my mother wanted me out. She'd had enough. It was

Saturday morning, the twenty-second of September, and the day began with a gesture of kindness. Mom said: "Good morning."

"Good morning," I said, as though saluting a passing ship.

Then she asked me if I needed to go shopping.

"Shopping?" I thought this must be a trick.

We went to the mall that morning and by noon were coming home with bags of new socks and underwear. Once we were home, Mom said that I needed to clean out my drawers and straighten up my room.

I asked why I had to "clean out my drawers." It didn't seem that she was aware of the meaning of her words.

"We are starting over." That afternoon, Mom called the house from her office phone. My mother told me to leave, to get out of the house, *that night*. She was polite, but she was firm. "Go somewhere else," she said.

"Are you kicking me out?"

"Doesn't that relieve you?"

"Sure, Mom. Anytime." I hung up the phone and was filled with an instant chill.

When Joe came home, he saw me packing a tote bag. He got upset and tried to stop me from leaving. I told him to talk to Mom about it, but he called our father instead. According to Joe, if I took the car, the Chevy, I'd be stealing the other half of it from him. He thought I wouldn't know better. Joe handed me the phone. Dad was on the line: "Son, it's your choice. Either you stay at home or you spend the night in jail."

"I think you should call the police, Dad, so I don't get too much of a head start."

"Boy . . ."

"Have me arrested. Do you think I care? I would rather spend the rest of the year in jail than continue to live in this house, and can you blame me?"

"Suit yourself," he tried to say, but I'd hung up the phone.

When I emerged from my room, Joe was at the other end of the hall. There was no point in fighting, and there was no point in negotiating. Our standoff had come to an end. Now only our portraits stood between us, his on one side, Joe calmly smiling, and me, a *total maniac,* on the other. Months ago, I had taken my mug shots out of these picture frames and replaced them with graphic, surreal self-portraits that I'd done in class. I planted my radio against the wall and walked down the hallway, knocking all of the picture frames to the floor. Joe stared, and I walked out of *the cave* with a journal, a tote bag, and a radio.

About ten minutes into my release, the engine blew and I coasted the car into a gas station on Seventh Avenue. While it was being looked at by mechanics, I could do little more than sit on my trunk, write in my journal, and watch the traffic heading to and from my old neighborhood.

I named the car. Its name was Puke:

> Here I am hottest day of the year sitting on the trunk of Puke with my radio next to me. My car and I are off to the side of 7th avenue. The car didn't make it three miles before it overheated. Writing or trying to write the thoughts that are popping into my head. Like the fact that I might forget this day, or from here on it's either a rags to riches story or just rags.

I planned to sleep in my car, but tonight I felt I needed someplace to stay. There were friends with whom I had collateral. I could call in a few favors. I flipped a coin, calling heads and tails for my two surest options. Marc won the toss, so from a pay phone I called him, the Dodo from *Alice in Wonderland*. He and I had become better friends in Kansas.

He told me that he could help me out later but he had plans to go dancing that night with a small group of our classmates. He was going to a nightclub in Fort Lauderdale, an all-ages show. "You can come if you want to," he said. By nightfall, after the car had been fixed, I parked on the street outside of the nightclub. I walked in and found a room full of kids in psychedelic T-shirts, jeans, and sandals, spinning and dancing. The black lights made the clothes and eyes of all the dancers seem brighter. My head spun. The music was pulsating, but I wouldn't budge. I walked slowly through the group, feeling estranged. I hadn't come to have fun, but now I felt like I was going to fall off the face of this earth.

The next morning I woke up on Marc's floor. As soon as the sun rose, I got up and left the house. It gave me a real awkward feeling to depend on other people this way. I drove downtown for a greasy breakfast, all my clothes rolled up into one bag.

Over my lunch break at work, I sat down in the stockroom and called my father from the office telephone. I don't know why I called, except that I thought I could earn his sympathy. It was a lost effort. I asked him if he would consider giving me the child support money that he was supposed to be giving my mother. I needed to raise money for a security deposit on an apartment. I needed someplace to live, I said, raising my voice.

"You have someplace to live."

"Dad, I can't live there anymore."

"That's why you called? No 'Hi, Dad, how are you?' "

"Dad, it's important. She told me to get out."

"Your mother tells me you're not doing well."

He wasn't listening. "She wants to hospitalize me. Did she tell you that?"

"No."

"She's lying to you too, Dad. She lies to everyone!"

"How much money do you need?"

"Three hundred and fifty dollars a month."

"What would you do with that?"

"Three hundred dollars would cover rent, fifty dollars for groceries. That's all I need, Dad. I have a job! I'm making money!"

"Sorry, son. Call someone else."

The office door opened, and I found my boss, Julio, standing there with big eyes. He said I couldn't "do that here." The whole conversation could be heard through a vent on the sales floor.

"Sorry, I really won't do it again."

"No. You can't. I'm serious."

"You mean I'm fired?" Our talk had gotten too heated.

"Yep. That's what I mean."

"Julio, you can't do this to me. I really need a job now."

He gave me this look like he'd been there before; he knew how I was feeling. "One week," he said.

I took a pill and went back out on the floor.

♦ ♦ ♦

I'd parked on a pier behind the Hard Rock Cafe, a strip of broken asphalt that extended out into Biscayne Bay. The pier doubled as a port for small private boats that came in and out of the harbor. It was not an official parking lot, so I didn't think I was breaking any laws.

After work that night, after getting fired, I climbed into my car and shut the door. I turned on the engine, and then I turned it off again. Having no place to go, I climbed into the backseat, collected my clothes into a ball, and used them as a pillow. I went to sleep that night on the pier, listening to the water gently licking the seawall.

Overnight, the sky had become a sheet of coal, and water came down in thick globules, pebble-sized raindrops that pelted the bay and splashed the windows of my car. Storm winds and seawater came in from the Atlantic, hurling spray. Pools of water wafted back and forth over the roof and hood of the car.

I rolled down the window and stretched my fingers out into the rain. I rinsed my eyes and shook out my hair. The storm was not in me. At home, I imagined that my room was empty, my breakfast free. I wasn't running away, I'd been told to leave. I turned to my journal and tried to think of what I could write about this. Could I describe my anguish? My confusion? My disappointment? Could I explain my mother's hypocrisy? I looked down at the blue lines on the pages and followed the movement of dripping water from the windows behind me. Nothing came. I had nothing to say. Voiceless, with a clear mind, I climbed into the front seat of the car and started the engine. I wiped down the inside of the windshield with a handkerchief, turned on the wipers, and drove carefully back to school.

When I got to class, I wore the rain on my face. I came into first period thirty minutes late and was met with jealous glares. Mr. Suarez said nothing and dismissed class early. "Your Government papers are due tomorrow," he said. "If you haven't begun yours yet, it will be obvious. So, do your best. This paper will go to twenty percent of your cumulative score. Think of it as one fifth of the year's work. *Comprende?* Any questions? Get out of here." The others rose from their seats. *"Get lost!"*

I went upstairs and stepped into the offices of the theater department. Dr. J was there, and we got to talking. I was exasperated. My four monologues had been washed out because of the medications I was on and the headaches I was having.

"This is only the beginning, Trav."

"Of *what*?"

Dr. J said, "I know how it feels, and yet, you have to believe me—*I have a few years on you now.* This is the beginning."

I broke down in his office, exhausted. Dr. J closed the door and sat across from me, behind a desk. He told me that another teacher, David Kwiat, had talked of taking me out for lunch, *his treat*.

"Really?"

Like Ellen Davis, David Kwiat was a voice coach. No matter what we had to say, he wanted all the students to open their mouths and be heard. In class, it seemed his only word was *clarity*. "Clarity is purpose," he said, "in the theater."

David Kwiat was also a writer, a poet, Dr. J told me. "You should talk to him about your writing." I could barely keep my eyes open.

Then Dr. J went on to say that I should check in with Jane Weiner because she had begun exploring a program for restaurants to underwrite students' lunches. If the plan worked out, I would have a different restaurant hosting me five days a week for a meal.

"You will get through this, but you have to accept that you are only at the very beginning of this process."

"Is there anyplace I can lie down until third period?" I asked him.

Dr. J walked me down to the teachers' lobby. The steps I took behind him were cautious. He filled a cup with water and opened a door adjacent to the lobby, marked LIBRARY. Most of the space inside had been taken up by a single table and four chairs. The walls had been built out with shelves. As the building was new, the library had not yet been completed. Nothing was organized or alphabetized. On the shelves were piles of plays, biographies, histories, and an assortment of theater criticism—some of which had been written by Dr. J. I closed the door, threw my book bag under the table, and crawled beneath. Bending my knees around and through the legs of the plastic chairs, I found a way of lying on my side, my journal and a handful of plays stacked under my head as a pillow.

CHAPTER TWENTY-TWO

Helter-Skelter

That afternoon, I called Jorge from the store and asked him if he could help me write a research paper.

"Now?"

"It's due tomorrow."

"*Okay.* I'll help you—but only if you don't mind if I practice piano while you work." I arrived so tired that my eyes were beginning to fail. I was standing back on my heels. I couldn't blink. Jorge let me in and made me a cup of coffee. I *reeked*, he said, and let me take a shower. Then I sat down in front of his computer, my eyes barely open.

"Okay, how many pages does the paper have to be?"

"Five pages."

"Easy."

"It's due in seven hours."

"Don't worry about it."

"Why not?"

"It won't help you." Jorge set up a new file for my paper and began by forming the header with page numbers. "Who is the paper for?"

"Mr. Suarez, Government."

"Type your last name here."

I pecked out the letters of my last name.

"What's your paper on?"

"Anarchy."

"Do you have a title?"

"No."

"Okay." He handed me the mouse. "What is anarchy?"

I typed: *Anarchy is.*

"Yes. Go further."

I typed: *Anarchy is an idea like communism or capitalism. It is the only political philosophy that claims to be the best and only enduring form of government for all people. Under capitalism money is the total force of politics. In communism people are the source of all the power and therefore are the most important resource. It is the people who make the world go round, the people who work and create value—*

"The proletariat," Jorge interrupted me.

"The what?"

"That's the name they used for the working class."

"Right, the working class, exactly."

I typed: *In anarchy, money is an abstraction because an anarchist believes that people are united by another principle.*

"What is that principle?"

Nature, I typed.

"What is nature?"

Anarchy.

Throughout the night, Jorge counseled me: "Who has written on this subject before?"

"It doesn't matter. Anarchy doesn't need to cite its sources or pay for another person's intellectual property."

"How about Emma Goldman or Rosa Luxemburg? What did they say about anarchy?"

"I haven't read them."

"You should have read them. You have to try to separate their writing from your writing, and your writing from their writing."

"No, I don't."

"That's what a research paper is, Travis. There are rules about how to do this."

"Rules about how I write a paper on anarchy?"

"There are no rules to anarchy, but there are rules to writing."

"What are you saying? I have to write on anarchy for someone who—"

"Does not know *anything* about anarchy! What can anarchy be compared to?"

"People think anarchy is chaos, but that's wrong. Look at

all the wars we've had. Look at Iraq. Governments fight, and fail; that is chaos. By what rule do we have to go to war?"

"That's good. Start there."

I turned to the computer screen, looked at the keys, and froze. "What did I just say?"

"Governments are wrong because governments fail—"

We did this until about three in the morning. At one point, Jorge tried to explain distance. He used the terms *objective* and *subjective, what happened* and *what happened to me*.

"So, even an anarchist needs to operate within the rules of society? But an anarchist means to transform society."

"True."

"But doesn't that also mean transforming grammar and language, because aren't grammar and language part of the system of *rules*?"

"Even the most radical thought"—Jorge was translating something in his head—"abides by the rules of common sense. Same goes with music."

"Music has rules?"

"Yes. Laws of acoustics, melody, harmonics. Think about rock 'n' roll. What's your favorite song?"

"Helter Skelter," I said. "The Beatles."

"Okay. Well, like any other song, it has a chord structure—actually a really simple one—and it is only because it lives up to this structure that the song is 'Helter Skelter.' If it doesn't live up to the structure, it becomes another song. That's a rule." He sat at the piano. "How does it go?" He set his fingers on the keys.

"When I get to the bottom—"

"Yes, yes. I think the song's in G." Then he sang: "When I get to the bottom I go back to the top of the slide . . ."

I fell asleep on the sofa listening to Jorge play me a lullaby.

♦ ♦ ♦

When Mr. Suarez received my paper the next day he raised his bushy eyebrows, a look of surprise on his face. I slept through the rest of class. After school, I went in to work wearing the same clothes I'd been wearing the day before. Julio opened the door slowly, unsure if he should even allow me inside. I told him to be honest. If he didn't want me to come in, he could tell me what to do instead. Then my boss said something wise: "In life, I try to look at the bad things like they're good things. Don't worry about getting fired. Get a better job instead."

"Where?"

He told me that he had a friend at the Brazilian restaurant in the same shopping complex, and that if I talked to him I might get hired.

"Who do I talk to?"

"Antonio."

After my shift, I walked straight over to the restaurant and introduced myself to Antonio. He handed me an application and a pen. I got nervous. He said, "I'm only hiring a busboy." He said he probably wasn't even going to read what I wrote down. "We just need to have the information someplace." I completed the form as quickly as I could and handed it back.

That night I slept on the pier, then on the beach, then in

the grove. I was on Tobacco Road, taking little pills from a jar. That week I made the acquaintance of other homeless people, people who'd been living outside for years. One of them, Bo Spider, seemed to understand my situation implicitly. "Some people come in with too much knowledge, spinning ten swords and promising disaster," he said. "No one can tame them, or tell them what is real. The trick is to become an orb and a wand at the same time, an individual." He had careful visualizations of these glowing orbs. He handed one to me like it was a magic bean in a fairy tale.

The next week Mr. Suarez started class with a discussion of our research papers. He began handing them back, from the highest grade to the lowest grade, and when he got to the bottom of the pile I was still empty-handed.

"What happened to my research paper, Mr. Suarez?"

"I don't have your research paper, Mr. Culley."

"Where is it?"

"It didn't receive an F, Travis. It got no grade at all." The class laughed at me.

"What didn't you understand?" I asked him, offended.

"I think I understood okay. The problem was your paper. It didn't say anything."

"You can think what you like. In fact, that's exactly my point, and exactly what my paper said. In anarchy you can do and think what you like."

"What did your paper say? I'm sure the rest of class would be interested to know," Mr. Suarez challenged me. "What is anarchy, Mr. Culley?"

"Anarchy is not a political system in the way that we have been discussing political systems."

"No? And why not?"

"Because it has no rules. It is what all political systems are fighting against: unruly, lawless, nature."

"And what is nature?"

"Selfishness, and adaptation. Survival. Man-made laws are only disciplinary conventions; markers and tactics. They are not necessary to the order of civilization, only to capitalism."

"So, nothing is better than something?"

"Nothing is better than something that fails."

He seemed to appreciate this, but the class was stunned. Mr. Suarez sat on the edge of his desk. "So, what does no system look like, because when I tried to read your paper, there was no . . . Forget it—there was no sense there."

"It doesn't look like this," I said, gesturing about at the classroom and his stack of papers.

"What does it look like then?"

"It's more obvious, immediate. The truth doesn't hide."

"How does society function?"

"People work together when they need help. If a bridge needs to be built, all of the people lend a hand. We identify dangers. We teach other people what they need to know. Community is what you call it when people help each other—when they cannot do something alone."

"How? How do we accomplish this adaptation?" He was pushing.

"Well, I'm adapting. You're adapting."

"But how? How are we doing this? Give me one example."

"An example?" I saw through Mr. Suarez. "Well? How do you adapt?" I asked him. I felt like I'd been strapped to my chair and surrounded by a room of fools.

"An example! One!"

I stood up and threw my desk into the air. Now Mr. Suarez had something to adapt to. The chair and desk, all chrome and plastic connected by a hinge, squeaked and spun mid-flight, attempting something of a pirouette. Mr. Suarez raised his arms to the windows and leapt like a goalie. The desk crashed to the ground and bounced in three directions.

"Leave!" He shouted over the commotion. "Go now!"

I grabbed my tote bag and left.

That night I slept on First Street, near South Pointe Park in Miami Beach. It was a short night of rest because I was now working later, busing tables. The next morning I had to have a meeting with Mr. Seidenman, one of the school counselors, about the incident in Mr. Suarez's classroom. I complained that Mr. Suarez had been making fun of me. He'd shown me disrespect in the classroom.

"Is that true?" Mr. Seidenman asked Mr. Suarez.

"Yes. That is true," he admitted flatly.

I told the story. "He didn't return my paper because he said he *couldn't* read it. He asked me to defend a paper he thought didn't even deserve an F. I threw the chair only to make an illustration, and I did not throw it *at* him."

Mr. Suarez's eyes bulged. "Where did you throw it?"

"I threw it in front of you, Mr. Suarez, only to defend my thesis."

"You had a thesis?"

"Adaptation."

He looked away and gave a big sigh. "You nearly gave me a heart attack!"

"I'm sorry, Mr. Suarez."

That afternoon, Michael woke me up in fifth-period English. Someone was saying my name. "Culley? Mr. Culley?" I looked up to see the other school counselor, Mrs. Anders, in the doorway, waiting. "Five minutes, Mr. Culley?"

"What is she talking about?"

"Go outside," Michael whispered.

"Sorry about the interruption," Mrs. Anders said to the class.

"That's okay. You can have him, as far as I am concerned." Mr. Remis got a laugh as I walked across the room, my hair hanging in my face, wearing my torn jeans and painted shoes.

In the hallway, Mrs. Anders looked at me seriously. "I want you to know that you're not in any trouble."

I held my arms together and my chin to my chest.

"I know things are hard right now. I have to let you know that your mother called. She says you haven't been coming home. Is that true? Are you staying somewhere else?"

"I'm not going home."

"That's all right. You don't have to go home. If you don't want to be home, you don't have to go home. Your mother only wanted to know if you were safe."

"I'm coming to school," I said.

"I was a little taken by it, honestly," Mrs. Anders said. "I have asked your teachers about your attendance, and it looks like you come to school every day."

Where else would I go?

Then Mrs. Anders came close and whispered: "You have a family here now, Travis. Come to school for support. I want you to think of New World as your family."

On Monday morning, right at seven-thirty, I stepped into a little room on the administration floor. Mrs. Anders and Mr. Seidenman were there with the new principal, Mandy Offerley, and a psychologist, Bill Matts. Everyone was dressed for work, blouses and slacks. I arrived in torn jeans and painted shoes. Mother appeared, hair done. Father appeared, apologizing for his tardiness.

Over the course of a three-hour meeting, Mrs. Anders made it clear that as long as I stayed in class, the school administration would have no reason to have the state of Florida investigate my parents for neglect or abuse. What they would need would be proof that I had a stable address. If these two things were accomplished, my parents would not be held in violation of the law.

"Would that be all right for both of you?" Mrs. Anders asked.

"Well, um, yes," Mother stammered.

"Sure," Dad agreed. The room observed.

I sat back in my chair, prepared to cover my face as my parents nearly lost their heads in shame, or perhaps in gratitude.

To secure this commitment from my parents, Mrs. Anders had to determine how the school could be sure that I would not spend another night in my car. My mother arranged to help me look for apartments that weekend.

"I work this weekend," I said, looking at my feet.

"I'll get started on this immediately," Mom assured us.

"We need a date," Mrs. Anders restated.

"Saturday."

The next issue of concern was where the money would be coming from. I was impressed by the conversation because Mrs. Anders and Mr. Seidenman spoke right up about it. I saw my parents go back and forth, and then my father said: "There is the boat."

"The boat?" Mrs. Anders wrote in a steno pad.

Mother told the story: "In our divorce proceedings a budget was established for Travis's education that was based on the value of our old ski boat." I had never been told of this.

"How much is that?"

"Two grand."

"Excuse me?"

"Two thousand dollars," Dad said, more humbly. My father seemed a completely different man to me now. He looked down at the ground when he acknowledged me and his now ex-wife. Something had changed in him. He had no power over me. He had miraculously become the least fearsome of them all.

When all of the details had finally been settled, the adults stood up slowly from their chairs. I was the first out of the room, but Mother made an insincere show of inviting me home.

"The house is open to you, unconditionally," she said.

At work, I prepared things. I told Antonio at the restaurant that I would have to do a split shift or a long lunch on Saturday, that weekend.

"What for?"

"I have to see an apartment."

"*Okay,*" he said, "leave at noon and then come back at five. That should give you plenty of time."

"On Saturday?"

"*¡Sábado!*"

♦ ♦ ♦

As class let out on Friday, Dr. J took me aside and asked me if we could talk in his office. He was concerned about my writing.

"My writing? Do you mean my spelling?"

"Well, no. I can't read it. It is illegible, and that which I can read, frankly, makes little sense. I'm worried about your literacy, Travis."

"My literacy?" I said, thinking he might have said something different.

"You have to show it to me in your writing. You have to be able to put all of your thoughts and feelings down for another person to be able to see them. It is the most important thing that you can do, and the most important thing that you can probably take from New World School of the Arts."

"What should I do?"

"Well, you need to work on this, Travis, before you graduate. You have a lot of ideas, big ideas. People need to be able to hear from you. You need a way to express yourself."

"How do I do that?"

"You need to read."

"Books?"

"Yes."

"But how do you get through a book?"

"You just do—you focus on it and do nothing else, you look at every detail. Perform the words. Find some example for each of the different characters that you meet. Know what you know. Be patient. Look at the pages first like you don't understand any of it and wait until some part of it makes sense. Build on that part, and trust."

"Trust what?"

"Trust what you hear."

I felt like I was a ghost in the room, I didn't know where to go.

"Do you know where the main library is?" Dr. J asked. "Look for Hayakawa. S. I. Hayakawa, a book called *Language in Thought and Action*." He wrote down the name. "His book will take you step by step.

"You have to be able to write, Travis. Your thoughts are invaluable. Your ideas are unique, but you have to be able to express them in clear, sensible ways. You have to be able to explain yourself when it comes to your sometimes very complicated thoughts. You need to be literate so that there is no confusion about who you are, what you want, or where you are supposed to be going. If you cannot do that, you will find that other people will become more and more unable to help you."

"Is that what this is about?"

"Yes," he said. "All of us, everyone, we all want to help

you, Travis. But you need to focus your energy in the right places."

Dr. J never intimidated me. He had a natural way of teaching. In our discussions, it was like he was allowing me to see over his shoulder, check his facts, and ask him questions. On a later occasion I asked him what else I should be reading, and he came to me with a personalized reading list of seventy key writers, everyone from Aristotle to Thomas Mann. Dr. J was an encyclopedia on the history of literature, film, theater, art, and music. He was also the author of a comprehensive multimedia humanities textbook called *The Art of Being Human,* which is in universities and colleges around the world. What makes his explanation of the humanities special is that he looks at the whole of civilization and describes each subject within its own history. There is a history of painting, a history of love, a history of technology, of death, of happiness, and so on. The book is not a rigid chronology because, as he explained to me, influence is not always chronological. Influences can be contemporary, historical, religious, or economic. "It isn't history we are trying to make," he says. "Art is not about breaking a record. Art gives us some way to believe the world will continue to change and have history."

♦ ♦ ♦

On Saturday, my mother picked me up from the restaurant, as agreed, and drove me over the MacArthur Causeway. At that time, this was where you could find the cheapest rent anywhere in Miami, and for good reason. South Beach appeared to be a ghost town whose sun-beaten streets were host to poor families and stray dogs.

For two hours we rode around on the sunset side of the peninsula looking at rooms and apartments that had been advertised in the classifieds section of *The Miami Herald*, and in every one I saw, my mother found fault. This apartment was too close to the highway. That was too much rent. This one had no carpet. They were all excuses.

"We have to find *the right one*, don't we?" she said.

"No. We have to find any one that you can afford given the terms of your divorce."

When she spoke with landlords, she spoke in *us* language—"We would like to find a place for him to live"—and she drove me from parking meter to parking meter, jerking the car forward and back to keep from getting too emotional about what was going on. I saw her trembling with the quarters and the car keys. With each apartment we saw together, she seemed more fragile. "Home," she kept saying, as though it was a quality.

Then we saw an SRO, a single room, listed for $210 a month. It was a beige efficiency with a sink that jutted out of the wall. The floor was carpeted in a dark brown acrylic that seemed right for old offices. The room came furnished, and all of the utilities were included. There was a bed, a card table, a chair, a beige dresser, a bedside table, a small refrigerator, and a window. There was one light in the middle of the room, and it was either on or off. "This looks like a prison cell," my mother said, and I spoke up to sign the lease.

In front of the landlord, my mother begged me to reconsider, and I said, "No. I am living here."

"Well, tell me why. What do you like about the room?"

"It has a door," I said. "It's close to school, and it is cheap, so there won't be any reason that you can back out later. Are those reasons that you can accept?"

Mother wrote a check. I signed the lease, and the landlord, without a single word, handed me the key.

"Are you happy now?" Mother asked, bitterly.

"Take me back to work."

CHAPTER TWENTY-THREE

A Joker in Every Deck

The first weeks in my apartment were intolerable. I would have rather been in my car some nights. It was lonesome. I left the light on, sat up in the twin bed, and wrote in my journal until I fell asleep. I had no radio, no television, and no telephone. I listened to the passing traffic and a neighbor's air conditioner. Often, I would take my voices for a walk, find someplace to sit, and write a few of their words into my journal. I had many names for my journal now, my *log,* my *house,* my *cohort,* my *secretary,* my *calendar.* Some objects are called on for many things, and like people, they earn many names.

On Alton Road, I stole a construction pylon with an orange light and set it in the middle of my room, blinking. When I tried to sleep, I would sometimes not remember where I was. I missed my mother and my brother, no matter how much agony they'd caused me. I missed the sound of their voices, even when they were yelling. All I could do was write to console myself, to manage the silence. I needed my journal because without it, voices would fill all the available spaces in my mind and come rushing out in tears.

When I wrote, I always heard something. A voice was needed to guide my pen. Listening, I could begin to write incessantly, like Gene-John did, with a stream of words coming to my mind constantly. I wrote to myself to be my own company. I wrote to myself to give myself tasks, to tell myself to think differently. I wrote until there was no more room, not a single speck of white on the folio. If I could use every inch of a page, then I was surely an excellent writer.

I turned to my journal for many purposes that year. To remind me of where my focus ought to go, even if only to tell myself what I should be doing, I entered it into my journal. Embarrassing and gratuitous thoughts were entered without hesitation. Once in writing, they no longer burdened me.

I had written my way through the shoelace journal and two composition notebooks by the spring of my junior year. Some of the pages were so overwritten that they were barely coherent. I began looking for a new journal when I started running out of space in the last. This would be my fourth volume, exempting only the first attempt, and it would mark the fact that I had now been writing every day for the past eighteen months. I was through with composition notebooks, and with them I was through with lined sheets. Now my mind could rest only on clean sheets of blank paper in a good spine. I wanted a cover, a hardback, not just a collection of papers. I looked through a bunch of sketchbooks at an art supply store on Biscayne Boulevard. Most of them were black, but on the middle shelf, there were a few white canvas hardbacks. When I first got a glimpse of them, I snatched one up and held it to my chest. Behind the plastic cover there was a little piece of cardboard that advertised how I should use this book. "Paint me!" it exclaimed. I imagined it saying "Tickle me!" and knew that I would never want to touch it with paint.

I wanted my book to reflect me, naturally and sincerely. I knew that if I bothered painting it, I would be worried about keeping the painting. I decided to keep the cover white so that it would absorb every trace of the world that I was thumbing through. I thought the cover might end up stained, torn, and thereby reveal the truth of the book in my hand, the unadorned, authoritative personal archive.

I drove to the beach with my new book in the passenger seat, and when I got home, I brought it up to my room and set it on my bedside table like it was glowing.

I made a final entry in my old composition notebook and set it on a makeshift bookshelf next to my bed. This journal had become my sole companion since I left home. I had kept it with me everywhere I went. The open pages of my journal became something like a surrogate ceiling, which I would glare into before nodding off in the evening, wherever I happened to be.

♦ ♦ ♦

Around the middle of November, I walked down Lincoln Road after all the bars and nightclubs had closed. When I got to Euclid Avenue, I saw a way that I could shimmy up a pipe in the alley. I climbed hand over hand seven stories to the roof of the concert hall that was home to the New World Symphony. A stream of drunks and partygoers were milling about for taxis below. I sat down on the ledge of the building, my ankles hanging off of the side, my journal and a pen awaiting inspiration to my right.

The sky was sparkling like a fine fabric with tiny mirrors woven into a divine pattern, now gently vanishing. The next day had begun to appear through this heavenly weave-work in tones of peach, pink, and blue. The lights from floating windows, streets, and the beams of passing cars, which had seemed all night to imitate the Milky Way, now resolved themselves into a vast array of buildings and roads that looked false to me, like they had been meticulously painted by the maker of some elaborate model. Each detail, meaningless in itself, was only significant as part of a larger structure.

I had been contemplating suicide—*a* suicide, not mine. I opened my book and tried to write something of a suicide letter for B.J. to see if there was any chance that I'd been wrong. Nothing came. My difficulty began with the fact that I still had trouble spelling the word: *suicide*. Besides this, I wasn't quite sure yet how I should feel about it. Its meaning understood—why was the word misused and overused? Who benefited from threats? I wondered. Probably no one. But who benefited from the suicides of other people, or from erroneous claims?

My mother, as I had suspected, was like the character in my play who had invented a suicide to accomplish another goal. She'd treated B.J.'s death like he wasn't her brother, like his death was only some warning for us about the dangers of excess pride or pleasure, some opportunity to say "I told you so."

To use words this way, I understood, involved a trespass of her brother's heart. To have endowed him with an intention, whether to ward me away from drugs or to set me on a regime of prescriptions, broke the Hippocratic Oath and disabled the last line of trust between us. Had he really wanted to kill himself, there would have been some corresponding sign, some impression that the result, his death, could verify. He would have expressed himself—before and after. But he'd made no threat, and he wrote nothing down. The radio he'd sent to my brother came without a letter or a picture or a set of instructions. If he had been feeling suicidal, even remotely, why would he not have sent that package with some reflection of himself, some clue that said: "Restore me"?

B.J. wasn't thinking about suicide. He was not on a ledge such as this one I sat on. He had a family he came home to every night. People were counting on him. I knew, given the most remote chance of suicide, my uncle would have written *something*.

Seeing this, I was no longer confused. My mother had her reasons for coming up with the story. In view of everything, in view of my whole confusing life and all of my unexpected obstacles, I had this: a pen with which to describe them. What Dr. Greenbaum had observed when he wrote about my "tenuous hold upon reality" may have been my mother's influence on me. His letter may have been a symptom of her messy excuse for a working family. I decided that night I would have to stop taking the antidepressants.

The sky changed, and the stars turned into specks. Chilled, I stood from the ledge. At sunrise, I left the building through an internal fire escape and stepped out into the sunlight carrying only my journal under my arm like a newspaper. I was cheerful about having succeeded on my journey that night. My uncle had spoken. There was a reason for writing and a reason for not writing. They *both* said something.

♦ ♦ ♦

When the stores opened on Collins Avenue that morning, I stepped into a dusty used bookstore as the shopkeeper was opening the door. I went down the aisles and started thumbing through the pages of bird-watching books, history books, and novels. I kept browsing the dusty shelves until I came upon a small red paperback in the philosophy section called *The Image: Knowledge in Life and Society*. It was a sociology text whose first chapter dealt with the theory of organization. Immediately, I had a number of ideas, strange and mundane alike.

I read the first page of the book, and then I read another. I read a third page, and a fourth; and I was amazed to find that I understood what this writer was trying to tell me—

four decades later. Each sentence seemed to take me closer to his worldview:

> *The meaning of a message is the change which it produces in the image.*

I bought the book for $1.75, and I set it down on the table in my apartment. How was the world organized? I had to force myself to find the answer, to search for the word for the answer. When it seemed that I had reached the heart of the theory, ideas balanced themselves and opened up gracefully. Each sentence led to a new conclusion. It seemed I could stand within the spaces it created. There were folds and faults that opened up to fissures, which fell on forever. I could walk through a sentence looking down, and then step around the bends of its construction. When I stopped I felt like I was spinning. I started writing in the margins, asking questions, confessing, at every point, my ignorance, my *dis*-organization.

If one idea was explained through the use of another, I found another book. I'd buy it, steal it, or borrow it from someone else's shelf, and even if I read only part of it, I kept it. I would soon find myself sprawled out on the floor, caught between the pages of ten or more books. I would leave the books open around me so I could compare the writers' contexts, hear their voices, and weigh their arguments.

A library began to grow in my room. For bookshelves, I piled together plastic milk crates that I had stolen from the loading docks of nearby grocery stores. For every twelve or fifteen books, I needed another crate. Consumed with questions and new ideas, I began to take long walks. If it was late at night, I sat at a table in the corner of a twenty-four-hour coffee shop and kept working, reading and writing.

Within only a few weeks of living alone, I had begun working on essays, poems, and an outline for a play. If my hand was tired, I opened the book by Kenneth Boulding and continued his lesson on the image. Then I found the Dhammapada, a collection of the Buddha's teachings. There was a chapter about the control of the mind, which I read about a thousand times. At the twenty-four-hour coffee shop I would read one of these books and write myself into exhaustion. All kinds of people would come through there: partygoers of every stripe, club kids, drag queens, tourists, cabdrivers, herbal medicine doctors. I found that the element of distraction tested my perception of what I was reading. If the authors were right, their sentences would prove true both in the context of their arguments and right there in the coffee shop, or wherever I had gone that night. Reading and writing for hours, sometimes until morning, I came to treasure my time living on the beach.

If I stayed in, I would turn all my lamps on until a warm glow surrounded me. I sat on the floor, books open, looking into myself as though I were only the contour of a cloud alive with *eidos*. When I became too tired to read, I curled up on the floor, listening to old philosophers surmise conclusions in the back of my mind. Closing my eyes, I let myself sprawl out on the open books, arms and legs creasing their yellowed pages, tearing their jackets, and bending their spines.

In the morning before classes, I kept writing. During my break at work, I kept writing. Backstage, between scenes, the same. I didn't have the four-colored ballpoint pen any longer, so I used better pens with finer points, and I bought them by the dozen: red, green, blue, and black. My entries became smaller. I thought this way I could ensure that they remained private. I would take efforts to make them impossible to read. Soon, the pages of my journals were saturated with tiny manuscript blocks of micrographic reflections. In them, I delighted that I would prove the mortality of countless ballpoint pens.

One night, I stepped into a beatnik coffee shop on Drexel Avenue and set my two books on a table. I nursed a cup of coffee and kept to myself, reading. Then I was interrupted by a strange-looking man with curly red hair and an unlit cigar hanging out of his mouth.

"What are you reading?"

"*Learning* to read."

"What are you learning to read?"

I slid the book across the table.

"Hegel? Silly self-consciousness! How did you get in there, my boy?"

Behind him, I saw a tall rabbi with a white beard. "Simcha, this young man is *learning* to read Hegel, and I think he has a question. Don't you have a question?"

The rabbi cast a long shadow over my journal, smiling. "Yes?"

How could I be so frank? "What does this word mean?" I pointed to the word—*phenomenology*—and Simcha stepped back.

"That's *his* domain."

The man with the red hair said, "*Pheno* means feeling, and this is a phenomenon because the feeling part of being is not particular; that is, it is transcendent. We are all feeling. It is a different question than what you are feeling, and it is still another question whether we all feel the same way. Phenomenology, after Hegel, is different from the phenomenology of Hegel because he was the first to bring this term into the discourse of philosophy. *Spirit* is a mistranslation, because the original German uses the word *Geist,* and *Geist* means 'mind.' So, the phenomenology of *spirit* is also the phenomenology of *Geist,* or *mind,* don't you see? And it would be a similarly fair question to ask whether or not the *pheno* of our thought—that is, the structure of our cognition—is alike. If it is, well then, my mind feels like your mind, and his mind feels like her mind, and through these deductive analyses we may arrive at the apperception that our experience is a universal experience, known as the truth: *self-consciousness.*" He peeked at the other open book on the table. "What do you have here?"

"That's my journal."

"You write awfully small. How can you read this? Simcha, have you seen this?"

"I can read it because I wrote it."

The weird guy broke into laughter and walked up to the counter for a refill. I looked up at the rabbi. "Is he a professor?"

"Used to be. Now that's what people call him."

"What's your name?"

"Simcha Zev."

"And what's with the robes?"

He smiled. "You have done a lot of writing, haven't you?"

"Not really. This is only the beginning."

"You're almost done with that book."

"This is the beginning of a much larger project—"

"Coffee, Nick?" The Professor asked.

From a table in the corner, a man with long hair and Indian robes said in a thick New York accent, "Sure, fuck it." More laughter. These three were too fast for any average society to know what to do with them.

Over the holiday season, which otherwise held little cheer for me, I sat and read at this little café quite a lot. I came to look forward to my next conversation with Simcha, Nicky Nicholas, and The Professor. They called themselves the Misfits, Simcha told me, and laughed about the levels on which the name rang true. Again, The Professor brought a cup of coffee to the Krishna devotee, then sat down at the weathered piano in the back of the room and started banging away at some classical tune.

"Rachmaninoff," I said. I recognized it from Jorge's fall recital.

Nicky looked up at me. "And he's trashing it."

"It's a lousy piano!" The Professor yelled across the room, over his own commotion. The wooden sides were splitting. The pedals could be heard pumping through the music. The Professor had to thump at the keys because a number of them were sticking.

"He's a madman!" I exclaimed.

"You should write that in your book," Simcha said.

The Misfits were older. They were on disability. They survived on Social Security. They ate at the same food banks.

They were not wealthy or successful. All three of them seemed to be on their last few dollars, always saving plastic spoons and napkins. I was also living under less than ideal terms, and so I fit in naturally among them.

Some days, The Professor would describe the fallacies of various philosophies and schools of philosophy, including Gestalt psychology and behaviorism. He'd say things off the top of his head like "The solution to the riddle of the origin is the phoenix!" The Professor had come up with a theory about *nongrammatical babble*. The idea was that you could write down all the associations your mind makes when you concentrate on a certain letter or sound, and enlighten yourself.

"Like Rorschach?" I asked.

He trumpeted, spraying water.

Simcha was also a visionary. He would walk the streets of South Beach with a sign around his neck reading ADVICE $1. He would stop and talk with anyone who had a question. I bought him many coffees on this basis. At a point before the end of school, our conversations had become so worthwhile that he suggested we find a carpet and set it out at Lincoln Road Mall. With a simple sign, we began inviting people to sit and talk with us. We called it the advice corner, and people put dollars in our cup as we spoke with them, offering our advice.

"All we need is the invitation," I'd say.

"All we have," he'd say.

CHAPTER TWENTY-FOUR

On Waking

I blocked out all of the light to my room so that I could bring the room to absolute darkness—even in the daytime. There was a metal shelf. It went on top of the dresser by the window. I added a hot plate and an electric kettle to the refrigerator in the corner. Seeing in a glance all of the objects in my room gave me a sense of confidence in my position. It gave me the decisive ability to focus. I could now read for hours without a single interruption. Of course, I enjoyed it. Reading was pleasurable to me because I was assigning authors to my voices, the same ones sometimes who would otherwise interrupt my teachers. Instead of getting distracted, I told the voices that I was reading about *them*. Suddenly they grew very quiet and began to pay closer attention. I was in control of the process now. I had enough money to keep from going hungry and some chance every other weekend of being able to fill up a shopping cart with groceries when my mom, now doting, would come by. Anyway, I had a job and a lunch card. I was guaranteed at least one meal a day. After work, I was tipped out by waiters and bartenders. I brought home forty to sixty dollars a night, much of which I spent on books.

Liz came to visit during winter break. She stayed a few nights. I showed her my favorite rooftops in South Beach. I had come to learn all of the best hangouts, sandwich shops, and parks that hid within the nightlife enclave. She brought me a few books she had picked up cheap at the university bookstore, including *The Birth of Tragedy* by Friedrich Nietzsche. I set it next to Rimbaud on my bookshelf.

Mom brought me Dad's old electric typewriter and gave me a radio. I set the typewriter on a desk that I had made with two bedside tables and a found piece of wood. I started writing little paradoxical poems, and short plays. Sometimes I broke into nongrammatical babble to merely practice typing, and to hear the sound of my typewriter.

♦ ♦ ♦

The first thing I did when I went back to school was visit Dr. J. I told him I was depressed and I wasn't sure exactly why.

"Are you able to concentrate?"

"Yes, like never before."

"So, you really did need to get out of your situation?"

"Yes, but now I need to get out of the apartment." Dr. J found this amusing. I told him about the books I had been reading. I checked out *The Use and Misuse of Language* by S. I. Hayakawa.

I had even found a book that Dr. J had written called *Identity Through Prose*. I showed it to him, curled at the edges, annotated and underlined.

"Do you have a job right now? Are you working?"

"Yep. Five nights a week."

"You know that we're auditioning for the main stage production soon. Are you going to be too busy to participate?"

"Probably."

"Can I give you something to look over?" He didn't say *read*.

"Sure, what is it?"

Dr. J handed me a piece of paper. On it was the monologue of a beastly prince named Segismundo who had been locked away in a cave and raised by animals, all because of one bad omen. A seer had foretold that Segismundo would become a tyrant, and so the king sequestered his son, keeping him in a remote cave. He kept his son secret so that he could find another heir. The only person to communicate with Segismundo was a general who fed the unfortunate prince, and taught him to speak human language. He was given no comforts, no literacy, and so little contact with human beings that he could only briefly learn from them. Dr. J said he was a Spanish Renaissance version of Tarzan, who learns from his circumstances, and in so doing teaches. The play was called *Life Is a Dream*. "Maybe you'll find it," he said, "interesting."

At first, I thought it was a bit overdramatic: "Heavens above, I cry to you in misery and wretchedness!" As the speech went on, Segismundo compared himself to a bird, a beast, a fish, and a river, asking why they were free when he, a man, was not.

That day, I took a nap under the table in the library, curled up on a pile of costumes, the script open in front of me. I repeated the lines over and over again: "Heavens above, I cry to you . . ." "Heavens above . . ."

♦ ♦ ♦

"Mr. Culley?"

I woke up in fifth period with Segismundo's speech crumpled up on my desk. "I'm sorry, Mr. Remis."

"It's time we talk about your research paper."

"I didn't write a research paper, Mr. Remis."

"*That's good,* I haven't assigned one yet."

The class laughed.

"You are to write a paper. It can be about anything you have read in class thus far." Then Mr. Remis went into a deeper voice: "Seventy percent of your grade will be based on what you turn in. You *must* take it seriously."

I folded up my monologue, trying to make this problem appear simpler. Mr. Remis threw his scarf over his shoulder and described what he wanted to see in our papers. "Only your best writing," he said, "and, Mr. Culley—*something I can read.*"

In my little room on West Avenue, I did not work on my paper. Instead I continued looking at Segismundo's speech, counting the rhymes and beats, breaking down the monologue. I made dinner with the text next to me, opening cans of tuna and mixing it into a bowl of rice. The more I got used to the emotions in his speech, the more I knew I would become able to voice my own: "Oh, Misery and Wretchedness!" Late at night, I walked up to the golf course on Twenty-first Street and I climbed trees, reciting the most difficult lines: *a bird, a fish*. I perched atop the roof of the Cameo Theater and read from *Life Is a Dream*.

At the audition, I held it crumpled and folded, still unsure if I had any idea of what Segismundo was supposed to look like or act like. Suddenly I looked out at the room of students. Who were these people? And why were they here? Why were the lights on? The class grew quiet. The words weren't coming. I turned to the piano in the corner of the acting area and pulled up the key guard. Then I made it howl, pressing down on all the keys I could cover with one hand. I turned the piano on its wheels to make a cave, an organ-like cave that moaned and croaked with octaves as far apart as I could reach from underneath. Pressing on one pedal, I began reading: *A bird, a beast, a fish, a river . . .* At the end of the piece I stood up from behind the humming piano, and the whole room sat back. I had grasped the essence of this heart-wrenching, enigmatic soliloquy.

A month later, I looked around to see that everyone had changed. Nerdy kids had turned into gothic punks. Preppy kids had turned into hippies. Half of the school had come out of the closet. All of the students, in one way or another, had embraced the idea that life was art if that's how you lived it, and that learning depended most on playing, on having your own approach to the material. It does not matter where the journey began, or where it leads.

"Mr. Culley?"

Oh no. "Yes, Mr. Remis?"

"What do you think of what we've been discussing?"

"Not much, Mr. Remis. Sorry I . . ."

"Michael, how about you?"

"Well, it's like Travis was saying, I think. The story ends without any promises."

"That's right. It's Hemingway."

"*And* it means that this is the world, at times abruptly cut off or . . ." Michael went on.

"Truncated," I added, helping.

"Yeah, that's it. The ending is truncated."

"Okay, nice. So by next week let's read the assigned pages of Eudora Welty's *One Writer's Beginnings.* The handouts are up on my desk; please take one as you leave today. Class dismissed." I left without my copy.

The year was winding down now. Opening night was getting close, and all of my class assignments were due. Finals were being scheduled, and still there were performances to see, and recitals to attend. Again, I asked Jorge if I could come by so that I could use his computer. I liked hanging out there because his mom was in publishing and had a wall of fascinating books.

After rehearsal, he helped me chop out nine and a half pages on the education of Segismundo. I wasn't exactly fulfilling the assignment. I wasn't writing about James Baldwin, or Ernest Hemingway, or Borges. I wrote my paper on what

I had been doing in class. Between this play and my journal, could Mr. Remis say it wasn't true? I turned my paper in on time with the other students, knowing that I was only accomplishing the assignment. It had the right number of pages, enough words, a handful of footnotes, and a bibliography.

♦ ♦ ♦

The play begins with Marta and Mandy, their hands and feet gathered in a massive net. They speak their lines while falling, arm over arm, to the floor. This is how the two travelers find Segismundo, bound to a chain. I open the scene with my mournful plea to the heavens: "Oh, Misery . . ." These are the words I recite every morning. The audience is captivated, the backstage crew is still. A giant clock moves slowly back and forth, upstage. I descend, hung by my waist. A small river runs beneath me in the cave. In the water I see my reflection—Dacyl.

In the second act I wake up in a royal bedchamber, surrounded by nurses and maids. Unknown to me, this is the day the king will test the oracle. Given the rashness I display, and my appalling lack of restraint, the king believes the oracle to be correct. I am put back to sleep, and returned to my cave. By the last scene, I have been freed from my bondage. I have led an uprising and forgiven my father. Now, the marriage. Marta is downstage-left, I am downstage-right, and the whole crew takes a bow together.

CHAPTER TWENTY-FIVE

Recognition

On the Tuesday before graduation, Mr. Remis posted the results of our papers. I went to the board. There, on the bottom of the list, was my student number: 7813357; in the other column, an F.

Mr. Remis said I could talk to him after class and I said, "No thanks." There wasn't anything to talk about.

On graduation day, I stood with the other students in a line outside of school. I kept my head down and I held my journal clutched underneath one arm. I expected Mr. Remis to see me and pull me out of line, but as the students began to walk toward the graduation ceremony, I walked with them. Inside the theater, I sat down with the others, wearing my cap and gown.

Valerie, once the flower girl from middle school, now made the valedictorian address. John Emerson was salutatorian. Jorge graduated fourth from the top of the class, and I graduated 109th, third from the last name on the list. After seeing my performance in *Life Is a Dream*, Mr. Remis must have decided to change my grade.

After the ceremony, I chose to continue on at New World. I entered the college theater department and began taking classes toward my BFA. I built sets. I wrote plays, and directed them. I finished school acting onstage with my teachers and, in my own time, filled books with tiny blocks of writing.

Years later, while reflecting on my journal, I began turning the pages of one volume around, looking at the entries upside down and sideways. It was then that I first had a sharp and painful memory about a boys' cabin in my youth. It was a terrible realization. I sat back from the page and looked at the shapes I'd made as if I had opened a familiar door, but inside of it now lived a nightmare.

I saw the ink, my own hand, words written into a macabre architectural matrix. There were panels, beams, windows. Every block of text on top of another as though built in a room of bunk beds. The fold was the ceiling of the cabin I had woken up in.

All of my time writing, I had been unconsciously rendering the confusion of waking up at church camp. To see the journals right, I had to step away from the page and discontinue reading. I needed to look, and that alone was enough. Here it is, the ceiling itself:

People. oh, Jesus, people. I found extremely appealing [illegible] statement to the idea
we speak about what we know, what we are and those things which concern
example; John and I having a conversation about psycology I brought up the ab-
dity of their idea of psycosis and of course he brought up the absurdity in their
of neurosis. At that point in time I didn't pick up on the clue but still be sure to
time. This was brought to my attention by my theater teacher "Elle" in a small dis
of my impersonation of John to class in his absurd (this absurd world!) in his
mannerisms. In the improv. I wonder — I must correct my English! Again! I
improv I showed John reading a book in an empty room, waiting for some
appearance and afterword in a re-imitation as I related to her, John's ch
ter just flowed out of me which was rewarding. Liz. I saw her today in her
shirt and cut off jeans. By no means of course would she even keep up the
or was she, by another way? well I asked — no — I said "Liz, we're gonna have
talk." (Her) "About what?" And then I said "oh, come on don't be ridiculous. Thi
very fucking strange, so we're going to have to talk." "Ok, well how about now?" "I ca
now. I've got to go but when I've got time and you're around, we'll talk" and she
and in some kind of sirical tone of voice she walks away and says "you're so d
just like always!" and I got pissed at the Sue Culley way of winning an argumen
matter what it was she actually meant to say. Then she took her red "Bob" an
her knew [illegible] and twirled away. How do I feel about her? of course I

[illegible]

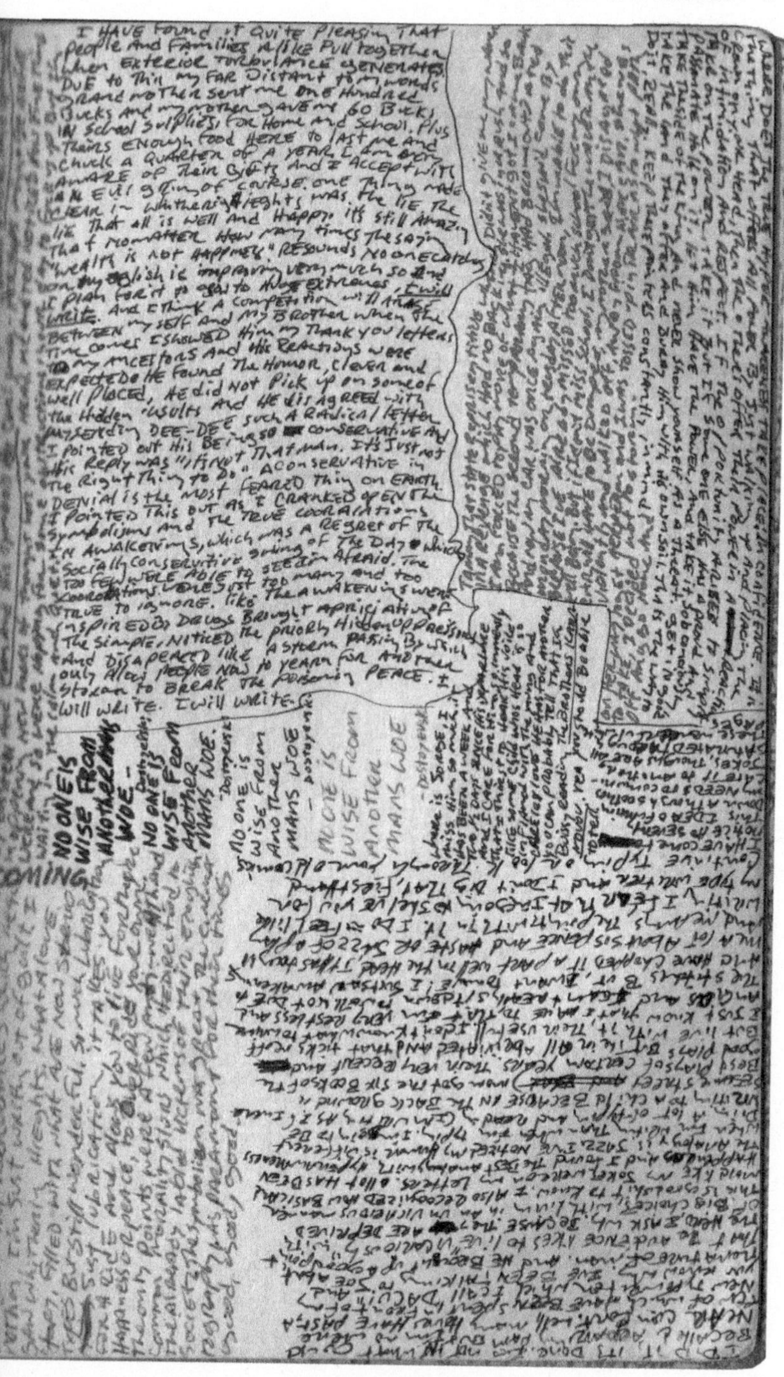

I HAVE found it Quite Pleasing That People And Families Alike Pull together when exterior turbulance generates. Due to This my far Distant [illegible] words grand mother sent me one Hundred Bucks and my mother gave me 60 Bucks in School supplies, for Home and School. Plus theirs enough food Here to last me and chuck a Quarter of a year, I am very Aware of Their gifts and I accept with an evil grin of course. one thing made clear in withering Heights was the lie the lie That all is well and Happy. its still Amazing that no matter How many times the saying "wealth is not happiness" Resounds No one ever catches on. my english is improving very much so and I plan for it to go to Huge extremes, I will write. And I think A competition will arise Between my self and my Brother when the time comes I showed him my thank you letters to my ancestors and his Reactions were expected. He found The Humor, clever and well placed, He did not pick up on some of the Hidden insults and He disagreed with my sending DEE-DEE such A Radical letter I pointed out His Being so conservative and His Reply was "it's not That man. It's just not the Right Thing to Do." A conservative in Denial is the most feared thing on earth. I pointed This out as I cranked open the true coorelations symbolisms and the true coorelations in awakenings, which was A Regret of the socially conservative swing of the Day which too few were able to see or Afraid. The coorelations were just too many and too true to ignore. like The awakenings were inspired by Drugs Brought appriciation of The simple, noticed the priorly Hidden oppression And disapeared like A storm passing By still only Allow people now to yearn for And never stand to Break the poisoning PEACE. I will write. I will write.

NO ONE IS WISE FROM ANOTHER MANS WOE —Dostoyevsky

NO ONE IS WISE FROM ANOTHER MANS WOE. —Dostoyevsky

NO ONE IS WISE FROM ANOTHER MANS WOE —Dostoyevsky

NO ONE IS WISE FROM ANOTHER MANS WOE —Dostoyevsky

In 1994, I graduated with a BFA from New World School of the Arts. My girlfriend Lenyr helped me pack boxes full of plays that I had either read or performed. I packed the library: Aeschylus, Euripides, Goethe, Marlowe, Molière, Kleist, Beckett, Albee, Shaw, Mamet, Shepard, all of the great avant-gardists, like Brecht, Jarry, Handke, and Breton. In another box: Kant, Marx, Machiavelli, Barthes, Bakhtin, Merleau-Ponty, Hegel, Sartre, Foucault, Adorno, Deleuze, and Guattari.

Before I left Miami, I made a stop at Simcha's apartment. He lived in a blue building on the second floor. He never locked his door. He asked, how would anyone find his shower if he locked his door? He had no furniture, not even a chair. He had no television or radio. He kept a pot of kosher rice and vegetables warm so that anyone in need of a shower or a meal could come to him and find them for free. I knocked on his door, but I heard nothing. I thought if he wasn't home I would just leave a note on the windowsill saying goodbye, but the door opened and I saw the face of my friend. He was sad, I could see.

"Have you taken a vow of silence?"

He had nothing to say.

"I'm leaving, Simcha. I wanted to say goodbye."

He shook his head.

I had a pen, and held it up. Soon we had a large sketchbook. He wrote down the reason for his vow. I wrote down that his heart should be lifted. Simcha had become my teacher. I wrote down what I'd learned.

What will you do? he wrote.

Theater, I hope. Maybe I'll be a writer someday.

He smiled.

For the rest of the afternoon, we sat in his living room writing down our conversation on large sheets of paper, setting the papers out on the floor around us. By the time we came to *Good luck and be safe,* the floor had been covered. I left him to gather up the notes of our uncommon friendship.

In Chicago, I did a fair amount of wandering. I appeared an introverted writer trying to tap into the city's theater and performance art scenes. It wasn't quite what I'd hoped. I remember looking at the city with fresh eyes, astonished by how much could happen in one place and time. To me, the city was a single cohesive work of art, a great coordinated dance. I had to experience it at very slow speeds initially because I found this effect so profound. I used to walk about with pennies, and set them heads-up at the very ends of sidewalks, between the cracks in stairs, on streetlights and curbs. Often I had no one to talk to and no one to see, and so I opened myself to being a public citizen who saw people of all kinds. I found that I enjoyed going to cemeteries for solitude. The feeling of walking among all the etched statuary was no different from that of walking down Michigan Avenue. In the same way, I was reading all of the signs available.

The Winter Garden on the ninth floor of the Chicago Public Library was a sanctuary for me. There, I would spend my afternoons if I didn't have to work at the bookstore in Evanston. Soon, I requested all of my Tuesdays off because those were the free days at the museum of the Art Institute of Chicago. I would divide up these days into three parts. I would spend the morning at the museum while it was quiet, then I would have lunch at a nearby deli and write an entry in my journal. After lunch, I would pack up and spend the afternoon on the top floor of the library with the play that I was writing. I read plays, studied ancient Roman history, and, eventually, I discovered the zip code demographics guidebook for Illinois. Like I said, I'm fickle. After a few months studying this, I began reading about Chicago. I had found my own Mount Olympus, from which the whole world seemed to easily come into view.

Between the library and the museum, I wrote a number of plays, some of which are very long and most of which are impossible to produce. I founded a theater company, which folded after two productions. In 1996, I organized a bike art show for the Critical Mass bicycle ride and from there on found myself among the riders. I wrote a memoir, *The Immortal Class: Bike Messengers and the Cult of Human Power,* about my rookie year as a bicycle courier in Chicago. After the book's release, I settled for a part-time job at a bookstore and a part-time job as a messenger. Everywhere I went I kept a journal with me. When I had a minute, I took notes on life. I began to write in clean, easy, balanced lines. As my life slowed down, I decided to go back to school.

I continued writing poetry and reading philosophy. I expanded my journal volume by volume as I worked in various art-related jobs. Delivering my application to the School of the Art Institute of Chicago, I wasn't sure what I would uncover, but in my first year, I began confronting the memories that were waiting for me in my journal, carefully preserved, waiting for a safe time—and a safe place—to be accepted and understood.

♦ ♦ ♦

On February 15, 2003, after protesting the rush to war in Iraq, I made a call to my old mentor, Dr. J. He answered and said he was going to bring me to Miami, expenses paid, to be acknowledged as alumnus of the year and recognized for my "exceptional achievement" at an annual gala performance that pulled together a sampling of current work being done across all disciplines.

On the night of the gala, I wore my best shoes. I met with students and toured backstage, meeting the school's next graduating class. Students ushered the audience to their seats. I walked down the aisle to the second row and found a seat next to Dr. J and David Kwiat. It was reserved for me. I sat next to my mentor, program in hand, my journal in my lap. The night began with a song. If I closed my eyes, I could hear Liz Brownlee. More curtains were pulled back, opening to a series of vignettes, sketches, operettas, and musical theater scenes. Andy Noble had directed *Six Characters in Search of an Author* by Luigi Pirandello. Dr. J nodded to me as the piece came to a close and applause filled the theater. It was intermission, and that was my cue to head backstage. I stepped into the little hall that led behind the wings, reminded of past productions, gala nights, and my own graduation, all of which had taken place on these very boards.

To my right was Jeff Quinn, the set designer. Farther back, at the old light board, were Dan Palmer and Larry Miller. These were the guys who taught me how to build stages in college. Jeff gave me a congratulatory nod, which also meant "Get up there." Then the spotlight came on and found the three top representatives of New World School of the Arts onstage. There was Dr. Pellosi, the president of Miami Dade; Ellery Brown, the principal of New World's high school; and Patrice Bailey, now dean of the theater department.

Mrs. Brown began: "Every year, when the time comes for the Rising Stars, we are confronted with some essential questions, like: Why do we do this? What is the purpose of this school? And what, every year, do we hope to accomplish? The selection of the alumnus of the year goes a long way toward answering that question. *Travis,* could you come out here, please?"

Patrice gave me the nod, and I stepped out onto the stage. A microphone was placed in my hand.

EPILOGUE

Dear Aneta,

On December 16, 2003, my grandmother gave me the full story: Right after my parents separated, she thought it was time to bring her son, B.J., and my mother together. She thought, this way, they could help each other at this point in their lives. Both families were in trouble, ours already divided. Days before my uncle's disappearance, my grandmother secretly mailed B.J. a ticket to fly from Seattle to Miami International Airport. On the twenty-sixth, the day after Christmas, he was scheduled to land. This was why he had sent the mysterious radio weeks earlier. There had been no note in the box, but for a very good reason. He had intended to install my brother's radio himself. Besides, my mother's gift was to be their reunion, and he did not want to spoil the surprise.

When B.J. went missing, my grandmother held her tongue. Initially, she didn't know why he had not made his flight. She only knew he hadn't. I asked her about the possibility of suicide, and she flatly denied it.

"Joelle called just before the holiday," she remembered, "asking if she should increase his medication." Grandma had been a nurse all her life, but she wasn't familiar with this new generation of mood stabilizers. Grandma told Uncle B.J.'s wife that it would *probably* be okay, but was unable to imagine what would happen next.

"The ticket was in his glove box," she supposed, "the night B.J. left his family."

When his body turned up, she buried the story about his visit, and the ticket she'd sent him. Her surprise had backfired horribly, and none of the details mattered now. I think she couldn't bring herself to explain the scope of the tragedy.

In some way, this was all happy news to me. I'd learned that my uncle had been on his way to help us pick up our lives right in the heart of my mother's "Dark Years."

♦ ♦ ♦

In the time that it has taken to answer your question, I have read *Pride and Prejudice.* I want you to know that I troubled over these characters a great deal, and their choices. I loved the writing, the acerbic British humor. I read over the correspondences many times. While I was expecting the story of *Pride and Prejudice* to be a diversion, and a comedy, I never imagined that it would lead to a relationship of letter writing.

When we left that little bookstore and went walking through the city, you told me that you wanted to introduce me to a friend of yours. You led me around the monument to Alexander, and pointed up the marble stairs of the Helsinki Cathedral. The sky was clear. We could hear the boats creaking and knocking together in the harbor. I followed you. I stood with you outside of this astonishing temple, admiring the friezes, pillars, and domes. Then, reaching for the door, you found that it was locked. You read the sign, translating from Finnish: "Closed for Renovations." You looked at me with so much to explain.

I remember you saying before you returned to your classes that literature could be thought of as a modern form of scripture. The stories we create are revealing, enlightening, and redeeming. "Literature fills our lives with art, poetry, ethics, and morality," you said. I could not disagree, but only add that you might approach the problem of *literacy* more simply—even with a blank page and a pen. Objects teach. Look into things. They will tell you what to do with them. If you look closely, they will tell you who you are.

ABOUT THE AUTHOR

TRAVIS HUGH CULLEY is the author of *The Immortal Class: Bike Messengers and the Cult of Human Power.* In 2003 he was named Theater Alumnus of the Year by New World School of the Arts. In 2006 Culley completed his MFA in writing at the School of the Art Institute of Chicago, and he was a recipient of the Ox-Bow Fellowship in Saugatuck, Michigan.

www.TravisHughCulley.com

ABOUT THE TYPE

This book was set in Sabon, a typeface designed by the well-known German typographer Jan Tschichold (1902–74). Sabon's design is based upon the original letterforms of sixteenth-century French type designer Claude Garamond and was created specifically to be used for three sources: foundry type for hand composition, Linotype, and Monotype. Tschichold named his typeface for the famous Frankfurt typefounder Jacques Sabon (c. 1520–80).